Growing up in
THE POST-WAR
FORTIES

Nance Lui Fyson

Batsford Academic and Educational London

Typeset by Valentine Press Ltd
and printed in Great Britain by
R. J. Acford Ltd.,
Chichester, Sussex
for the publishers
Batsford Academic and Educational,
an imprint of B.T. Batsford Ltd,
4 Fitzhardinge Street
London W1H 0AH

Frontispiece: **(1949) A member of the Rodney Youth
Centre in Liverpool planning his next piece of
mischief.**

Acknowledgments

The author and Publishers thank the following for
their kind permission to reproduce copyright
illustrations: BBC Hulton Picture Library for the
frontispiece and figs 2, 4, 5, 6, 10, 11, 14, 16, 19, 20, 21,
22, 23, 24, 30, 31, 32, 33, 36, 37, 38, 39, 41, 43, 44, 45, 47,
48, 49, 50, 51, 53, 54, 57, 58, 59, 60; and The Photo
Source Ltd for figs 1, 3, 7, 8, 9, 12, 13, 15, 17, 18, 25, 26,
27, 28, 29, 34, 35, 40, 42, 46, 52, 55 and 56.

Contents

The Illustrations

1 War Ends—but Problems Remain

Hard times continue

"Don't you know there's a war on!" This was the explanation for all the hard times and shortages in the first half of the 1940s. The Second World War ended in 1945 but hard times continued throughout the decade. A much-heard expression was, "Well, you know

1 (1946) This swing frame was made from sections of a Morrison shelter. (Morrison shelters were strong steel tables under which people could huddle for protection as bombs fell during the war.) After the war, shortages of materials meant that old shelters and other wartime equipment were used to make everyday items.

how difficult things are...". A newspaper "Saying of the Week" in 1947 was a quote from a ten-year-old girl: "When will this post-war be over, Daddy?"

The war had ended but reminders were everywhere for years. Michael Taylor (b.1936) remembers German prisoners of war coming to help dig the garden just after the war. "They used to do odd jobs. I was fascinated but I think my mother minded having them around." Michael Taylor also remembers going to his father's office in the City of London. "In the area north of St Paul's Cathedral there were acres of rubble, nothing but rubble." When

visiting his grandfather on the Sussex coast he recalls enormous explosions as beaches were cleared of mines and tank traps. "It was well into the late Forties before things got back to normal in that area."

Michael Storm (b.1935) began travelling into Hull just after the war to go to school. "I took the bomb sites for granted. There were lots of big spaces, hoardings, corrugated iron. Because I grew up in the country I didn't have a clear idea about what might have been there."

A reminder of the war to London children was the wire and wooden fencing which enclosed city squares in 1948. These fences were much less elegant than the iron railings which had been there in the 1930s. The railings had been taken down so that the metal could be used in the war effort.

Things did return to normal after the war, but it took time. One newspaper columnist wrote in early 1946: "The pattern of life improves each week, though still inconspicuously....We forget when we shop how much we may buy that once was beyond dreams: hairpins, powderpuffs, even sixpenny combs, an electric iron, an aluminium pan....There are oranges here and there off the ration...."

Bridget Hastie-Smith (b.1932) thought that the period after the war was almost worse than the war in some ways. "Because the war was over you rather *felt* things should be very much better than they were. Then in the late Forties things did actually start to get better." Valerie Knight (b.1931): "It was really like the war after the war."

"Challenge to British Grit"
Britain was involved in the whole of the Second World War, from September 1939 to August 1945. Over 400,000 British lives were lost. Michael Storm (b.1935) was one of thousands of children who spent the post-war

2   (1949) Cricket being played on a London bomb site. The sign was part of a government campaign to increase production and exports.

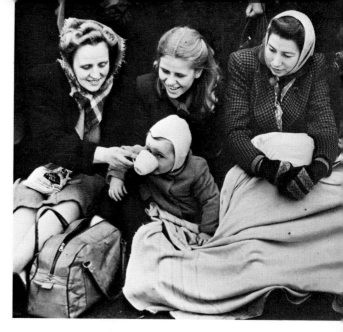

3 (1947) 20 November was Royal Wedding Day for the Princess Elizabeth and Lieutenant Philip Mountbatten R.N.A. Thousands of people (including many well-wrapped children) spent the night before camped on the Mall, London, to be sure of a good view on the day.

Forties in a single-parent household. (Michael's father was a merchant navy captain lost in a North Atlantic convoy in 1942.) Worldwide, over 40 million people had died as a result of war, with millions more homeless.

Six years of war had left the country drained. Britain was on the winning side but ended the war £3,000 million in debt, with exports down to about one-third of the pre-war level. In 1945 Britain was still one of the world's "Great Powers" but the slip into second rank was starting. The country was virtually bankrupt, with the largest debt of any nation in the world.

Government advertisements encouraged the public to increase production and exports. In one 1947 advert, called "A Challenge to British Grit", the government explained: "Eightpence won't buy a shilling's worth of goods. But for every shilling's worth of cotton or rubber, tea or food that we get from abroad, we had only eightpenny-worth of exports to offer last year. The rest we are getting on tick. Now you see why we must export one-third more this year and still more after that."

Aid to Britain
Lend-lease aid from the USA had been vital to Britain's economy since 1941. This aid stopped in August 1945 as fighting ceased. Britain's economic crisis was then made worse by the conditions of a post-war American loan. The situation was very serious by 1947. America therefore announced more aid to Western Europe under a "Marshall Plan". Over $11,000 million was provided from April 1948 to the end of 1951. Britain was a main receiver of aid (second only to France) until the end of 1950. Marshall Plan aid helped to keep Britain going. Without this aid, Board of Trade

officials estimated in 1948 that rations of butter, sugar, cheese and bacon would have had to be cut by one-third. Cotton goods would have virtually disappeared from British shops. The shortage of timber would have meant only about one-quarter as many new houses being built.

European co-operation
The experience of war left countries anxious to build better links. An Organization for European Economic Co-operation (OEEC) was formed in April 1948. This was a forerunner of the Common Market. The North Atlantic Treaty Organization (NATO) was formed in 1949 to increase security for the countries of Western Europe, including the UK.

Loss of Empire
Britain's Empire in 1945 was still much as it was in 1919. However, over the next two decades the Empire rapidly became much smaller. There was a growing demand for independence on the part of colonized nations. (For example, India, Pakistan, Ceylon and Burma all gained independence in 1947/48.) It was also true that the Second World War left Britain financially drained and unable to support the high costs of running an Empire. There was, too, a growing loss of will.

4   (1949) Children of West Indian immigrants with their English friends in Liverpool. Britain has had immigrants from all over the world for many centuries. In 1948 a British Nationality Act was passed declaring Commonwealth citizens "citizens of the UK and Colonies". As British passport-holders, these people had the right to come to Britain to live. Britain was desperately short of workers and *encouraged* immigrants to come. Factories, building sites, the new National Health Service, transport—all needed more labour. It was not until 1960 that restrictions started closing the immigration door.

In July 1949, London children and adults were shown exhibits to better inform them about "the colonies". This "Colonial Month" came after a Colonial Office survey had revealed the public to be somewhat unaware. A survey of 2000 adults found just less than half able to give the name of even one colony. About 3 per cent even thought that America was still part of the Empire!

World events in the headlines seemed far away to most UK children. Some things, however, did make an impression. Michael Storm (b.1935): "I recall the assassination of Gandhi in 1948. [Mahatma Gandhi led India to independence in 1947.] The name was unusual. I didn't really understand."

The new Labour government

In the early summer of 1945 Conservative Prime Minister Winston Churchill dissolved the government. This had been a coalition, governing since 1940. The Parliament that was dissolved in 1945 had been elected ten years earlier with a strong Tory majority.

The result of the 1945 election was a landslide victory for Labour. People hoped for better times. An election victory cartoon in the *Daily Herald* of 17 July 1945 showed a man, woman and child. They smiled as they climbed a hill into the sun. In the dark valley behind them were storms of "slums", "oppression", "fascism" and "fear". The cartoon caption said "FORWARD – AND GOODBYE TO ALL THAT!"

Labour's election programme, "Let Us Face the Future", set out proposals for increased nationalization of industry and an expansion of the "welfare state" (a phrase coined in the 1930s). This meant an increase in the range of services offered by both central and local government to help with individual social problems.

There had been government intervention in almost every area of life during the war. Afterwards, Britain never completely went back to the lesser government involvement of the 1930s. An important trend since the war has been increased government activity in the economy.

5 (1947) Throwing snowballs outside Buckingham Palace. This was the coldest winter since 1881 and caused much hardship. However, children and others did have some enjoyment from so much snow. At an army camp near Cheltenham, Polish soldiers built a large snow figure of Winston Churchill, complete with cigar.

Some key politicians of the time

Winston Churchill (Conservative) was Prime Minister 1940-45 and became Prime Minister again 1951-55. During the years 1945-51 he was Leader of the Opposition.

Clement Attlee (Labour) was Deputy Prime Minister in the wartime coalition government 1940-45. He led the Labour government as Prime Minister from 1945-51.

Ernest Bevin (Labour) was Minister of Labour and National Service in the years 1940-45 and became Foreign Secretary 1945-51.

Aneurin Bevan (Labour) was Minister of Health 1945-51 and Minister of Labour and National Service in 1951.

Stafford Cripps (Labour) was Chancellor of the Exchequer 1947-50.

Herbert Morrison (Labour) was a Cabinet Minister 1940-51, and Deputy Prime Minister 1945-51.

2 Family and Home Life

Changing homes

The end of the war meant a different home for many children. Some returned to their real homes, from families with whom they had stayed as evacuees. However, many of these children no longer had a real home to which they could return. (Over 4 million children were evacuated during the war. The idea was to move them to areas where they would be safer from bombings.)

Sometimes whole families had been moved. Michael Taylor's (b.1936) family had been evacuated from their Surrey home at the outbreak of war because they lived so close to an aerodrome. The house was used by troops. The family returned in 1946 to find their home "pretty badly written off. It was totally overgrown".

Housing shortages

Housing was one of the issues most worrying people in post-war years. During the war almost 4 million houses, about a third of Britain's stock, had been damaged by enemy action. Of these, nearly half a million had been totally lost. Many thousands of people were homeless or living in very cramped conditions.

Children were used to seeing half-built houses after the war. There was a great shortage of building materials and problems of distributing whatever there was. The aim was to build about 200,000 new permanent dwellings every year. The government managed

6 (1949) One family solved their housing problem by living in a barge on the river near Oxford. There was still a desperate shortage of homes.

only 550,000 by the end of 1949. About 125,000 temporary houses were also erected and over 140,000 damaged houses repaired.

By 1951 Britain was still short of about 1.5 million dwellings. Ten million households in England and Wales were still living in overcrowded conditions, substandard or unfit houses. (The comparable number was down to 2.7 million households by 1976.) The Housing Act (1949) introduced the idea of improvement grants paid to home owners by local authorities. This was to help encourage more repairs and better maintenance of buildings.

It was common for couples to start married life living with in-laws or other relatives. *The Picture Post,* a popular magazine of the time, in 1946 featured six families who lived as one. The children from all the families had their own quarters in one wing of the house. The women took turns serving them meals and the parents otherwise shared in caring for them all.

Pre-fabs

Prefabricated housing was erected. These "pre-fabs" were meant to be a temporary measure, but thousands were still standing in the early 1980s. One of the most heavily bombed areas, Bromley-by-Bow, had many pre-fabs put up in late 1945 and early 1946. The streets were named after former US presidents such as Franklin Roosevelt.

7 (1946) A Gloucestershire family moves into a new "pre-fab" home. These were meant as temporary housing because of the shortages, but thousands are still being used in the 1980s.

8 (1946) Two young London "squatters" carry out a precious roll of linoleum. The family had just been evicted by court order. The housing shortage prompted many families to move into any housing space they could find, whether it was legal or not.

9 (1946) Sixty-six homeless families invaded a former US Air Force camp at Watford to turn the buildings into homes. They had no water or lighting at first but the Mayor of Watford visited and promised help. All the squatters were ex-servicemen or wives of serving men expected home soon.

In early 1946 one six-year-old girl living in a Franklin Street pre-fab had an important visitor. Franklin Roosevelt's wife called on the family for tea. One hundred aluminium pre-fabs were put up on the Addington Golf Course in Surrey in early 1947. Most of these were hardly approachable because of mud.

Squatters

In the summer of 1946 groups of homeless families began moving into the camps that had housed soldiers. By mid-August nearly 20,000 people had become squatters in these camps. Families who took over the former US Eighth Air Force Camp at Bushy Park near Hampton Court lost no time in completely redecorating. They turned the dance hall into a nursery where over 100 children were looked after during the day. Walls were painted to show circus scenes. In the evenings families used the hall for social events.

New towns

The New Towns Act became law in August of 1946. The idea of building "new towns" was to lessen crowding in major cities. Several new towns were begun in the late 1940s: Stevenage

(1946), Harlow (1947), and Peterlee (1948). Britain was already a very urban country, though less so than today. About 80 per cent of the late Forties' UK population lived in towns and cities, compared to over 90 per cent in the 1980s.

Tenure

In the 1930s only about 20 per cent of houses built were council-owned. In the post-war Forties about 80 per cent of houses built were council. The trend since the end of the war has been for more and more people to be council tenants or owner-occupiers, with many fewer people renting privately. The proportion of owner-occupiers was only about 26 per cent in 1947 compared to well over 50 per cent in the 1980s.

housing tenure	% 1947	%1980
owner-occupiers	26	53
council tenants	13	32
private renters	61	15

Baths and loos

In the late 1940s only about two-thirds of all homes had a plumbed-in bath. Hilary Strudwick (b.1939) had relatives with an outside loo. These were much more common then than they are now. "It was scary going to an outside loo when it was dark, right down the bottom of the garden." Valerie Knight (b.1931) recalls the paper shortages affecting supplies of toilet paper: "Families tore up old newspapers. We used old copies of *Who's Who*. It was a great joke in the family."

Household goods shortage

During the six years of war people had used less than three years' normal amount of household goods (furniture, bedding, cleaning tools, etc.). These were in short supply throughout the late Forties as well. A 1946 sale of A.R.P. (Air Raid Precautions) surplus stock was held at a depot in Brixton, London. All kinds of Civil Defence stock was being sold to the public. There were blankets, brushes, buckets.... Children as well as adults sorted through the piles.

There were endless advertisements like this one in 1946 for mattresses. The ad. said: "Sorry to have to say 'Wait for it'. Short of manpower, short of material, the output of Slumberland Utility mattresses is not meeting the demand...."

A 1946 Design Exhibition at the Victoria and Albert Museum was called "Britain Can Make It", showing design at its best. However, little of this was available for general sale. The exhibition was cynically nicknamed "Britain Can't Have It". An "Available Now" label on a piece of fabric or an electric iron meant the goods were in full production but still scarce. Demand for goods was far ahead of output.

Furniture

Furniture was still rationed until the end of 1950. Very basic "utility" furniture carried the famous utility mark. As with everything else, people improvised as best they could. Gerald Pudney (b.1944) recalls a bathroom corner cabinet which his father made out of old packing cases. "Wood was in very short supply."

10 (1946) Baby-minders look after some children. The well-worn furnishings are typical of those in many homes at the time.

Paint and floorcoverings

Children shared in all the shortages affecting everyday life. In 1946 wallpaint was available in only ten shades compared to fifty shades before the war (and hundreds now). Hilary Strudwick (b. 1939): "There was a sameness about things. We had to have a horrid green on the walls. Colours were not very exciting."

In 1947 the cost of new carpets made them outside the reach of most households. Linoleum was available only to the privileged few with permits. (During the war, and after, people applied for permits to buy certain scarce items. "Priority classes" were given preference. Those judged most in need were people whose homes had been bombed and those setting up home for the first time.) Hilary Strudwick (b.1939): "We didn't have many carpets or rugs. We had three or four rag rugs which we had made. You cut up extra pieces of cloth and hooked them through canvas."

Keeping clean

Children were used to the fact that even keeping homes clean was harder because of shortages. For spring cleaning in 1946 sweeping brushes and brooms were scarce and there were almost no mops to be bought. The quota of dusters and floorcloths people were allowed had been cut by half.

Appliances

Labour-saving appliances were much less common than today. Derek Walker (b.1934): "Vacuum cleaners were not universally owned. Certainly refrigerators weren't either. These were still a rarity where I lived [Northern Ireland]. We had only a cool larder with ventilation holes on an outside wall." (Food was often kept in a small wooden "safe" with a screen mesh door. Refrigerators had been on the market since the 1920s, but were owned mainly by richer families until well after the war. By the mid-1960s, still only about a third of British households had a fridge.)

Derek Walker (b.1934) also recalls the old heavy mangles through which washing was put to squeeze out water. "Another point was that people sent more things to an outside commercial laundry. These were then much cheaper comparatively. We sent things like sheets. The van came to collect and deliver. Laundries were used even by many people who weren't very well off." Sometimes these vans collected more than laundry. One day Gerald Pudney (b.1944) was out shopping with his mum. He was old enough to be difficult for her to carry. He sat down on the pavement and refused to go any further. His mother had to thumb down their laundry van to get them taken home. "She was not pleased about that."

In 1948, only about 4 per cent of households had an electric washing machine, compared to 73 per cent of households by 1980. Such machines had been on sale in Britain since just after the *First* World War, but were still not common in the late Forties. The models that were around were very cumbersome, with hand-wringers on the top. Michael Taylor (b.1936) remembers his family buying their first washing machine in 1949. "It was a monster of a thing that made a horrendous noise and used to walk all over the kitchen."

Synthetics

Synthetic materials for household goods were not nearly as common as they are today. Derek Walker (b.1934): "You didn't have washing-up bowls in plastic. You had them in enamel or something like that. You didn't have all the plastic utensils, plastic mugs. Wood and metal were much more in evidence in household things."

Fuel shortages

The harsh winter of 1947 was made worse by all the shortages of fuel. The on-going shortage of miners was the main problem. An early 1946 newspaper headline shouted "MINES NEED 100,000 MEN". Many people had to find their own coal. At Ilford, mothers and young children "mined" with pickaxes, garden rakes, iron rods and shovels. They dug their way through a frozen sports field where a layer of coal was buried.

11 (December 1946) This was the first Christmas the Russell family had spent together for years. The post-war Forties saw many fathers coming back from the services and many children coming back from temporary homes to which they had been evacuated, in safer parts of Britain. (Some children were still in their "evacuee" homes for years after the war, and some never returned to their own homes.)

12 (March 1947) Children helped search clinker heaps at a gasworks in Kent looking for coke. People were allowed to take away as much as 56 pounds of coke for the cost of a shilling. Fuel shortages were serious.

Michael Storm (b.1935): "In our Yorkshire village we improvised sledges to get the coal from the station which was a long way away. We'd sledge over the snow, which was at hedge-top level, to deliver coal to old people in the village."

Valerie Knight (b.1931) remembers her father in Surrey taking away old wooden sleepers from the railway lines for fuel. "He wrote asking if he could buy the old sleepers. They said no. We were so cold he went out and took some anyway. I expect other people were doing it as well. It was all you could do. There was nothing else to burn."

Hilary Strudwick (b.1939) remembers how cold their Manchester house was with no central heating and just coal fires, especially in the winter of 1947. "Bedrooms were very

cold. We'd try to get dressed under the sheets." She remembers all the commotion when the chimney sweep came to clear out the fireplaces. "It was a major event when the sweep came. Everything had to be cleared out and washed and put back. I recall him pushing his long sweep's broom up the chimney. The soot used to get everywhere."

By May 1947 people were being asked to cut by a quarter the amount of gas and electricity they used, compared with 1946. Ministry of Fuel and Power advertisements explained that, because of the war, there was a shortage of generating plant. "When all available generators are working, if people still continue to switch on fires and lights, then the only thing to do is to cut off supplies to some areas."

Marriage and divorce

People generally married at a slightly older age (on average) in the post-war Forties than in the 1980s. A famous wedding of the time was that of Princess Elizabeth and Lieutenant Philip Mountbatten R.N.A. in November 1947. But even a royal wedding was touched by the austerity which marked those years. Princess Elizabeth was given 100 clothing coupons for the wedding, her bridesmaids 23 coupons each and pages 10 coupons each. (The coupons limited what could be bought.)

There were many fewer divorces in the post-war Forties than in the 1980s. The peak of 60,000 divorces in 1947 was, however, *ten times* the pre-war figure. The Legal Aid Act was passed in 1949. This opened further the possibility of divorce to many lower-income couples. (Legal Aid helps to pay the court costs of people whose income is below a set level.)

Babies

1942 marked the first noticeable rise in the birthrate since 1880. A few years later there was a post-war "baby boom" until 1947, when the rate started to fall back. A Royal Commission on Population was set up in the late Forties because of concern that Britain's population might actually decline. In the late 1940s the average number of children per mother was about 2.14. (This had fallen to 1.68 by the late 1970s.)

13 (February 1947) Fuel shortages meant frequent power cuts. Many babies and children had their baths by candlelight.

3 Food and Drink

Post-war crisis

There was a general "world food crisis" after the war. Much agricultural land in Britain (and elsewhere) had been used for airfields and other military needs. Clearing more land for farming was a high priority. In the first part of 1946 Europe as a whole was already short of 8 million tonnes of wheat.

A newspaper commented in 1947 that "the scramble for food occupies the foremost place in our lives today...prices of vegetables are soaring." The heavy frosts and floods of recent months "have destroyed whatever small chance there was of our food ration increasing in 1947".

Coupons and points

Many wartime controls continued. Ration books had "coupons" which had to be used

14 (1949) A scout earns a "bob-a-job" by helping a mother with her shopping. Ration books and shortages went on for years after the war. The average consumption of basic food items in 1949 was lower than it had been in 1939.

when buying many staple foods. The amount of these foods allowed per person varied throughout the war and in the years after. A buff-coloured general ration book was issued for each adult and child over six. Children under six each had their own green ration book and were allowed less meat. There were other ways of controlling food as well. For example, a "points" system restricted such items as tinned foods and dried fruits. Each item was worth a certain number of "points" and people were allowed a changing number of points a week when buying these.

In the spring of 1946 the weekly rations of butter, margarine and cooking fat were actually below the wartime level. The 1948 weekly allowance per person (13 oz of meat, $1\frac{1}{2}$ oz cheese, 6 oz butter and margarine, 1 oz cooking fat, 8 oz sugar, 2 pints of milk and one egg) was also well below the wartime average. In November 1948 the bacon ration went down from two ounces a week to two ounces every fortnight.

In 1946 Bridget Hastie-Smith (b.1932) was at boarding school in Hampshire. "Our weekly butter ration was put in front of us at breakfast time and we had to decide how much to have then and what to save for later. For tea

15 (July 1946) Extra assistants were needed in this baker's shop to deal with ration books. Bread was being rationed for the first time. This lasted for two years. In the weeks before rationing started there was panic buying of bread and flour in the shops. "The women have gone mad," said one baker.

we had just enough jam for one slice of bread. After that it was just margarine."

Scarce fresh eggs were sometimes preserved in "waterglass", a solution of silicate of soda or potash. Hilary Strudwick (b.1939) recalls her mother doing this in a big old wash boiler. Her mother had managed to get a quantity of real eggs in Yorkshire. "That was marvellous. Quite a big event." (Controls on eggs, as well as on flour and soap, were not removed until autumn 1950.)

Chocolates and sweets
Chocolates and sweets were on "sweetie coupons", especially valued by children. Michael Storm (b.1935): "We hoarded those scruffy bits of paper." Michael Taylor (b.1936): "A bar of chocolate was a luxury."

Hilary Strudwick (b.1939) was lucky in that her grandmother sent her sweet ration to Hilary's family during the war and after. This gave them an extra ration. In Manchester "we had a little sweet shop, Mr Thomas's, round the corner. It was an old-fashioned shop with a wooden counter and all the sweets in big jars. He took a brass scoop and weighed the sweets on a little scale."

Bread and potato rationing
There was post-war rationing of some foods that hadn't been rationed during the war. In 1947 potato rationing began. Bridget Hastie-Smith (b.1932): "We had mostly mashed swedes instead of potatoes. If there were some potatoes they were mashed up with the swedes to make them go further."

Bread rationing began on 21 July 1946 and lasted until July 1948. Bread rationing meant that bread, flour, cakes, scones and buns were on a new restricting scheme called "Bread Units" (BUs for short). A child less than one year old was allowed two BUs a week; children aged one to five, four BUs a week; children aged five to eleven, eight BUs per week; adolescents aged eleven to eighteen were

16 (1946) A family at dinner. The average number of calories eaten per person per day in the UK was about 2850. By 1948 this had fallen to 2680. (The UK average in the early 1980s was over 3300.) Michael Taylor (b.1936): "I can never remember feeling hungry but I can remember having to eat an awful lot of very boring food. We were always told if we were still hungry to fill up on vegetables. We grew most of our own."

allowed twelve BUs a week, which was more than the normal adult ration of nine. (Some adults were allowed more than this, notably expectant mothers, female and male manual workers.) "Bread Units" were needed to buy certain foods. For example, two BUs were needed to buy one small loaf of bread and three BUs needed for one pound of flour.

Another fact about bread is that it was all brown, with an extraction rate of 85 per cent. (White bread has much more of the brown germ removed, and so is rated about 70 per cent.) This very brown bread continued even in 1949. Bridget Hastie-Smith (b.1932): "We put salt and pepper on to make it more palatable."

The start of bread rationing prompted one newspaper columnist to write: "I pity the poor woman who has a large hungry family on her hands this summer and not the means to feed them in cafes and restaurants once a day."

Restaurants

In early 1946 it was a fact that people could eat in restaurants without having to give up coupons. This matter was raised in Parlia-

ment, as many people thought it unfair. The Ministry of Food replied that the additional paperwork would be overwhelming. A main reason for keeping restaurants coupon-free was really the desire to attract tourists to Britain. This meant especially tourists from the USA where food was much more plentiful. As one newspaper said at the time: "Nobody can say that outdoor London today, shabby and war-torn, is attractive to the eye. Take away its hotels and restaurants and the effect on the visitor would be gloomy indeed." Britain badly needed tourists to bring money into the country.

There were, however, some restrictions on restaurant meals. Diners could have only three courses, totalling a cost of not more than five shillings (25p). Bread was counted as one of the three dishes during the period of bread rationing. The five shilling meal limit and restriction to three courses was not lifted until May 1950.

Shopping: shortages

Shopping continued to be a problem for years after the war. A woman reporter wrote in one newspaper: "One reason why shopping has become such hard work is that supplies dribble into the shops in tiny quantities.... No one – not even the shopkeeper – now knows when supplies will be in."

"Under-the-counter" referred to grocers offering special favours to particular customers. If a grocer did get in some tinned fruit or something else in short supply he would offer it (quietly) to his "regulars".

Children were certainly aware of all the difficulties of shopping for food and other goods. In early 1949 one newspaper reported on the way very young children in nursery schools were acting out shopping as they saw

17 (September 1948) This was Britain's first "help-yourself" or "self-service" store, at Wood Green in London. Shoppers gathered goods in a wire basket and then paid for them at a cash desk. Now very common, "self-service" was a novel idea from America in the late 1940s!

it: "Teachers report that small girls automatically form queues and, basket on arm, discuss health, shortages and the weather. And on reaching the 'shopkeeper' they automatically turn a shoulder on the others and in an undertone ask what there is 'under-the-counter'. It is a sad reflection on current life but it proves that four- and five-year-olds are keenly observant."

In 1946 one newspaper noted the complaint over how such luxuries as tomatoes, off-ration oranges or tins of fruit were being distributed. Shopkeepers could not get enough for all their registered customers and tried to be fair by allowing one pound of tomatoes or oranges or one tin of fruit per household. Large families felt this was not fair to them.

As scarce foods reappeared, children tasted some of these for the first time. Michael Taylor (b.1936): "I can remember very clearly having my first banana. That was 1947. I'd heard about bananas for years. Oranges were very short as well but we did occasionally get a few of those during the war."

Slower shopping, deliveries

Michael Storm (b.1935) remembers the weekly chore of going down to his Yorkshire village store on Saturdays for the family shopping. "There was this one shop. It got very full and everyone had big weekly orders. It was served by a gentleman with a very long apron. Everything was so slow because there were very long conversations. I remember leaning against the shelves waiting for my turn and staggering back all of two miles with the shopping."

There was less pre-packaged and processed food in the late 1940s than there is today. Hilary Strudwick (b.1939) recalls biscuits in large glass bins. Nearly three-quarters of all biscuits sold were not pre-packed. "You didn't buy packets of biscuits; shopkeepers would weigh out portions. You would say 'I'd like half a pound of this or that'. Sugar, too, was weighed to order and wrapped in sugar paper. Cheese and butter were also cut and weighed for each shopper."

Much shopping was delivered in the post-war Forties. Hilary Strudwick (b.1939) remembers the common system of order books. "Each week my mother wrote her shopping list in an order book. The grocer would get the things together and he would deliver in big baskets."

Drinks

John Owen (b.1940) recalls milk being delivered to his South Wales home. "The milk was in large churns and it was scooped out with a dipper. It wasn't delivered in bottles." Hilary Strudwick (b.1939) visited her grandparents in a Yorkshire village where the milk was delivered by horse and cart. "The milkman would ladle out a pint or half a pint. My grandmother always had her own jugs ready." In Manchester the milk was delivered in bottles with cardboard tops.

There was not the wide selection of soft drinks there is today. John Owen (b.1940) remembers liking lemonade. Michael Taylor (b.1936): "Tizer was the drink we always went for. A ghastly fizzy mixture." Even a year after the war was over beer was still very weak and a newspaper feature suggested making your own "Wine from Weeds".

Containers

One of the problems with food supplies in the post-war Forties was the shortage of containers. Britain could not afford to buy wood-pulp from abroad for paper and carton-making as she had done before the war. The packaging industry relied on the return of waste paper to make new containers. During the war people saved just about everything for recycling. After the war it was more difficult to get the public to continue this saving. In 1947 the salvage authorities were, as one newspaper recorded, "at their wits' end to get the co-operation they so badly needed".

Food parcels

Christmas 1949 was the best Christmas since the war for food supplies. Still, 750,000 food parcels arrived in Britain from abroad in the month before. Michael Taylor (b.1936) remembers packages from Aunt Edith in Boston USA. "There was great excitement over these." Hilary Strudwick (b.1939) also recalls with delight the parcels from relatives in America.

Unusual foods

The Ministry of Food tried to encourage people to eat some "new" foods to help overall supplies. Whalemeat was being promoted in 1947 but was not very popular. It was described as tasting like a "meaty biscuit". In April 1949 a newspaper columnist commented that "it seems that whalemeat must figure more prominently in our menus between now and the

18 (1948) Two Brownies try to pass their cookery test. The standard challenges such as "Make a milk pudding" or "Prepare and stew fruit" were altered to allow for the limits of what foods were available.

autumn. If we try we may be able to acquire a taste for it". (Whalemeat had in fact once been popular for royal banquets in Britain in the fifteenth century.) Michael Taylor (b.1936) remembers liking it: "It was rather like salty steak."

In October 1947 another unusual food was introduced called "snoek". This rapidly became a national joke. The snoek is a large tropical fish looking somewhat like a barracuda. The Ministry tried to encourage consumption of tinned snoek by publishing recipes such as "snoek piquante". By the summer of 1949 over a third of the snoek imported since 1947 was still unsold. In 1951 a large quantity of mysterious tinned fish appeared in shops. This was labelled "selected fish food for cats and kittens". Even with all the shortages people did not take readily to unfamiliar foods.

One unusual food that *was* widely used was "dried egg". This had been a basic food during the war when fresh eggs were short. In February 1946 dried egg was temporarily missing from the shops but soon reappeared and went on to "points".

"Food Facts" boxes

After the war, the Ministry of Food continued to publish "Food Facts" information boxes in newspapers. A September 1945 "Food Facts" box focused on "Making the most of Priorities for Children": "Young children have been given priority allowances of certain foods because they *must* have these foods if they are to grow up healthy and strong." Every holder of a child's green food ration book was entitled to a pint of milk a day. Children aged six months to two years had the special allowance of three shell eggs a week. Older children up to age six also holding the green child's book were still being allowed only packets of dried egg.

"Food Facts" boxes also told people as the rations allowed went up or went down. For example, a box in June 1946 announced a small rise in the sweet ration.

19 (1948) T. Wall & Sons invited 16 children aged 8 to 10 to taste novel dishes using ice cream (still in short supply). The comments were taken into account by the company in planning for times when stocks would again be plentiful.

Making do

"Food Facts" boxes encouraged hard-pressed mothers with ideas for making the most of what was available. One box suggested making "Barley Mince" – corned beef mixed with barley to make it stretch further. Another suggested cakes and puddings using no eggs.

In December 1945 a "Food Facts" box said: "This isn't going to be an easy Christmas but it *can* be a cheerful one...yes, you *can* still give the children an attractive party sweet that uses very little sugar." One recipe was for "Fruit Snow" and another was for "Rich Mock Cream" made with cornflour and milk.

There were extra rations of sugar, butter, margarine, meat and sweets especially for Christmas in 1945. With the food situation critical, the public was being warned not to waste bread. "Food Facts" recipes included "delicious dishes from left-over crusts".

Despite the problems, some of the dishes that were produced are remembered with pleasure. Valerie Knight (b.1931): "My mother used to make a delicious dish out of what was then fairly cheap, tinned corned beef. She'd grate carrots into it and make a sort of shape. It was lovely." Hilary Strudwick (b.1939) felt differently: "I used to think: not corned beef *again*...."

20 (1950) Rations of cod liver oil and orange juice for children aged one or two months to five years helped general health after the war as well as during it. In the post-war Forties over 12,000 distribution centres continued to distribute cod liver oil free of charge. There was a small charge for orange juice. Mothers used coupons in children's green food ration books to obtain these.

4 Health and Welfare

The National Health Service

An important achievement of the post-war Forties Labour government was the new National Health Service. An Act in autumn 1946 nationalized the hospitals and general medical doctors. The NHS itself began in July of 1948. The idea of such a free, comprehensive health service had been part of Labour Party policy since 1934.

Before the National Health Service began, about half of the nation's hospitals had belonged to local authorities. Standards of health care varied widely from place to place. Hospitals tended to charge patients according to their means.

In its first year the new NHS treated over 8.5 million dental patients and supplied over 5.25 million spectacles. There was a pent-up demand amongst poorer people especially. Before the NHS the poor could hardly afford dentists and had relied on Woolworths for eyeglasses. (You simply tried on pairs until you found one that made seeing easier.)

The National Health Service quickly became second only to the armed forces in the money and manpower it used. The Health Service was the largest single item in the civilian budget. Because the service proved so costly, in 1949 the Minister of Health accepted the idea of charging for prescriptions.

Health improved

Some diseases were much reduced or nearly disappeared as health care became more freely available. Diphtheria, tuberculosis, whooping cough and rickets have all decreased sharply in Britain since the Second World War. The dramatic fall in diphtheria between 1941 and 1950 was due to the immunization campaign which began in 1940. A whooping cough vaccine had been introduced in the 1930s but had no major impact until after the war.

21 (1948) A school matron weighs a pupil. In spite of rationing and shortages, people were healthier in the late Forties than ever before.

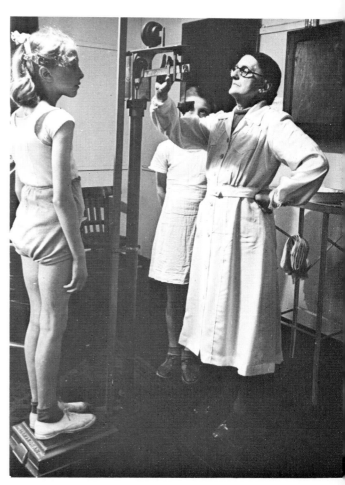

Medicines for children

"Milk of Magnesia" was one medicine commonly given to children at the time. A newspaper advertisement in 1946 showed a young boy: "Although wartime robbed him of many childhood joys there is one thing – good health – he did not miss thanks to mother. 'Milk of Magnesia' helped to keep him fit and free from stomach troubles throughout those anxious times. In the happier days ahead 'Milk of Magnesia' will remain your standby...."

"California Syrup of Figs" was also advertized: "Susan's vitality is amazing. She puts such energy into her play and never seems to get tired. When children are 'out of sorts' this natural laxative will regulate the system and put them right again."

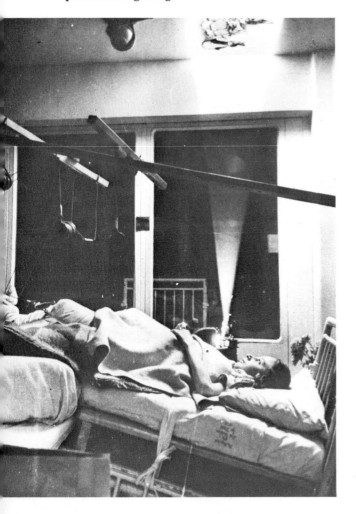

Infant mortality/life expectancy

The infant mortality rate began to drop markedly in the post-war Forties. There were still nearly 50 baby deaths for every 1000 live births in 1945. A survey in 1946 had shown that 65 per cent of mothers in the UK were without the services of a doctor at childbirth. They depended wholly on a maternity nurse. (The infant mortality rate was down to 12 deaths for every 1000 live births in the early 1980s.)

In spite of (and in some cases because of) rationing and shortages, British people as a whole were healthier by the late 1940s than ever before. Average life expectancy was about three years lower than in the early 1980s, but it was still higher than in previous decades. The percentage of the population over age 64 was only about 10 per cent in the late 1940s compared to 15 per cent by the early 1980s.

Rates of deaths from some causes (for example, cancers, motor vehicle accidents and suicides) are actually higher now than they were in the late Forties.

Some health issues of the time especially related to post-war problems. One of the effects of overcrowded housing was the growing number of home accidents. In 1946 one newspaper reported on the increasing number of burns suffered by small children. Many electric or gas fires did not have safety guards.

General welfare

The National Insurance Act of 1946 was another Labour government achievement. For the first time this brought the whole popu-

22 (1949) Great Ormond Street Children's Hospital, London. Machines from America allowed children to enjoy books projected on to the ceiling. The pictures could be changed just by pressing a button. Such machines were not made in Britain until 1952. (Parcels from America cheered other children in hospital. One ward in Southend Hospital received an unexpected gift of toys in 1948. These had been sent from a group of British war brides married to US soldiers and living in the States.)

lation into a complete welfare system. A Ministry of National Insurance was set up and a National Insurance Fund established. Employers and employees were to make weekly contributions. New systems of Maternity Grants, Death Grants and Family Allowances were organized.

An editorial in *The Times* newspaper of 5 July 1948 summed up public feelings about these changes: "Today the British public join together...for mutual support during the common misfortunes of life....The new social security system is, as the Prime Minister said in his broadcast last night, the most comprehensive of its kind ever introduced in any country....The new services treat the individual as a citizen, not as a 'pauper', an object of charity...the health service, like the social security system, the Education Act and so many other reforms can knit the nation together in a new way...."

Children's Act (1948)

The Children's Act passed in 1948 was another specific help to the welfare of children. The new Act provided for those children who had been included under the Poor Law (i.e. children removed from their home by court order either as offenders or as being in need of care and protection). The Poor Law was brought to an end in July 1948. One important part of the new Children's Act was to require local education authorities to appoint Children's Officers. (These existed until 1971 to look after the needs of children taken into care. They arranged for fostering and other alternative homes.)

The Children's Act was to help deprived youth. The National Society for the Prevention of Cruelty to Children was dealing with over 100,000 children a year at the time. Experts said that the number of children suffering from neglect or ill treatment was actually much higher. The estimate was that over 1 per cent of all children were "problem family children" — untended, undernourished, badly clothed and wandering as they pleased.

23 (1946) A mother draws her Family Allowance from a post office. These new allowances were part of the Labour government's legislation to extend the "welfare state".

5 Clothing

Shortages and controls

As with much else in the post-war Forties, clothing was neither bright nor plentiful. There were mainly basic "utility" styles. The coupons that controlled purchases went on until March 1949. Price controls on children's wear lasted until 1952. Most people faced the harsh winter of 1947 with shoes that leaked and well-worn garments. During the *six* years of war people used a lesser amount of clothing than they did in the *four* years before the war. Michael Taylor (b.1936): "I can remember my mother in the late 1940s getting a winter coat. It was the first time in eight or ten years – a tremendous event."

Michael Storm (b.1935): "I was only four when the war began so I was used to a certain austerity. Even after the war, clothes had to last a long time and you didn't have much of a change. You didn't really expect very much." Hilary Strudwick (b.1939): "There wasn't a great deal of choice and much more than now what we wore was decided by parents."

Four months after the end of the war the clothes ration was at its lowest ever. There were great queues in children's departments. Supplies of infant shoes and socks were less than half what they had been in 1943. "Demob" coupons were used to clothe some children. These coupons (which could be used for any civilian garments) were given to fathers as they were released from the forces.

24 (1945) A woman darns socks. There was much patching, mending and re-making of clothes. The shortages went on for years.

25 (1949) Children in the Cotswold village of Laverton learned to make their own warm clothes from wool left by sheep on the hedges. They made gloves, pullovers, scarves and socks from the wool they gleaned.

Baby clothes and nappies were very scarce, increasing all the problems mothers faced. It was mainly the women who looked after the family ration books and sighed as they juggled with coupons and points. A government announcement of 25 September 1947 was typical of those made weekly:

Take care of your 1947-8 clothing book. To save paper it will have to last you two years.

The 20 yellow coupons on page iii of the General, Child's and Junior Clothing Books become valid on 1 October for the five months ending 29 February next.

This is how they are made up:

16 coupons 'E' – value	1 = 16
1 set of $\frac{1}{4}$ coupons – value	1 = 1
2 token 'F' – value	$1\frac{1}{2}$ = 3
	20

Michael Taylor remembers the struggle parents had in those years after the war. "Fast-growing children could be seen in clothes that were ridiculously small for them."

Part of the problem was a shortage of workers. There was a national effort after the war to attract women and girls to the mills and factories. A newspaper in 1947 commented that clothes rationing would continue until many more workers could be brought back into the textile trade.

Another problem was the shortage of linings, highlighted by one newspaper in early 1946: "Our worn clothes would last longer if only linings could be replaced. It is lack of linings that has held up the shops' winter supply of coats and jackets and particularly boys' clothes."

26 (1947) A children's garden party in the grounds of St James's Palace. Little girls' party dresses often featured finely gathered bodices. Elasticated patterned stitching called "smocking" was popular, as were puff sleeves.

Making do

"Renovating" old garments was a familiar expression in the post-war Forties. Women's magazines were filled with ideas for "making do", in sewing as well as in cooking. People used whatever fabric they could get. Valerie Knight (b.1931) wore hand-me-downs from her aunt. "There just weren't the new clothes." In 1948, at the interview at her first job, Valerie wore her school uniform and short socks. "I hadn't anything else much to wear." Her white confirmation dress had been made from an old parachute. "You'd make coats out of blankets. They made everything out of anything."

Hilary Strudwick (b.1939) remembers her mother managing with great difficulty to get hold of half a parachute after the war. "All our petticoats were made out of parachute. She put on little shell edging to make them look prettier."

Black-out cloth was used during the war to cover windows so light wouldn't guide enemy planes to targets. After the war, the cloth was used for clothes and other things. Roger Iddles (b.1942) had a black-out cloth bag for holding marbles. Hilary Strudwick (b.1939) recalls black-out cloth "shoebags". "You had to have a bag to take your plimsolls to school for gym. Our bags were black." (Black-out cloth was another example of something that was *more* restricted after the war than during it. The cloth was coupon-free in wartime but in the post-war Forties went on the ration at two coupons per square yard.)

Boots and shoes

Shortage of shoes was a problem during the war and for years after. As Michael Taylor (b.1936) recalls: "Shoes had to last a very long time. One's feet were almost bursting out of the toecaps before there was any question of another pair. It wasn't in our case lack of money but just sheer shortage."

During the war the main problem was the shortage of sole leather. After the war the difficulty was supplying enough shoe uppers. In April 1946 the restrictions on shoe-making (but not repairing) were removed. Once again it was permitted to make such frivolities as high heels, open backs (called "sling pumps")

27 (1946) A group of boys in Cheltenham explain to a local Councillor their need for a playing field. Short pants were still the rule for younger boys. Michael Taylor (b.1936) had his first pair of long trousers at the age of 12.

and open-toed shoes. The leather for all shoe-making was, however, still very scarce. It was not until March 1947 that shoe repairers were allowed to cover the whole sole in leather (called "long-soling" by the trade). Many repairers still had only the materials to do a half-sole repair.

Parcels from Canada included clothing for the family of Valerie Knight (b.1931). "Friends sent my mother boots from Toronto. They sent one boot at a time so they wouldn't be stolen."

Stockings and socks

Stockings (often called "nylons") were in short supply for years after the war. In 1947 one newspaper described the supply as still "token". Valerie Knight (b.1931) recalls that as stockings slowly became more available they "were a purplish colour – and did they last!" Just after the war there were still American soldiers based near her school. "Girls at school were told not to walk unac-

companied in Bushy Park. The American soldiers would give you things. Some of the older girls got their stockings this way but I wouldn't have dared."

Bridget Hastie-Smith (b.1932) remembers the shortages as well. "It was a disaster when you got ladders because stockings were so hard to replace. Little shops started up which mended laddered stockings. It was really big business. I can remember seeing them in the window of the shops doing the repairs."

Heavier stockings were in short supply as well. Up until the war, socks for girls were

28 (1945) "Three simple styles for the Junior Miss" – as 16-year-olds were then called. Valerie Knight (b.1931) recalls teenage girls wearing styles like those worn by little girls. "At age 16 I was wearing an awful check dress with puff sleeves and pull bows. We never had a 'teenage'. We went straight from being children to going to work."

frowned upon as school wear. Girls were expected to wear cotton or wool stockings (in black, brown or fawn), even in warm weather. These came to half-way up the thigh and were held up by garters or suspenders. For games at school, even longer "gym stockings" were worn that came up under the knickers. Wartime shortages of these cotton/wool stockings prompted a switch to ankle socks. Headmistresses thought this trend would be temporary, but after the war many girls stayed with socks as part of their uniform.

29 (1946) A children's fashion show was held at London's Dorchester Hotel. In many places it was still not common to see women and girls wearing trousers. Derek Walker (b.1934): "Where I lived [Northern Ireland] it was disapproved of. That began to change towards the end of the 1940s. Dress was more formal generally. Many more people still wore hats."

Ankle-length socks for men had proved very unpopular. By January 1946 the Board of Trade was once more allowing men's socks to be the higher, mid-calf length. First arrivals in the shops were being snapped up eagerly for 2/7d (about $12\frac{1}{2}$ new pence) a pair, plus 2 clothing coupons.

The "New Look"

In 1946 rules on dress-designing became less austere. One newspaper columnist wrote: "To the customer it means that the skimpy look in clothes will go." In February 1947 a "New Look" fashion blossomed, creating quite a stir. At the time, most women were in square, angular "man-tailored" clothes with padded shoulders. Shoes were heavy, practical and masculine. Skirts were short and jackets long. The "New Look" was much more feminine, with curved lines. "New Look" skirts were very full.

Teenager Princess Margaret was one of the first to show the "New Look". This encouraged many followers. Valerie Knight (b.1931): "The Royal Princesses were about the same age as me. My mother used to dress me up in 'Princess Line' dresses and coats."

Bridget Hastie-Smith (b.1932): "In 1947 clothes started to become exciting again after years of being rather dreary. There was a girl at college who was the first person I saw in the "New Look". We all thought she looked lovely – very glamorous." By 1948 the "New Look" with its longer skirts was having some influence on children's clothes. Even toddlers' clothes became about two inches longer.

The less skimpy look extended to items like coats. The waist-length "jigger" coat came into fashion, hanging loose at the front with no fastening or just a single button at the neck. These coats had wide sleeves, deep cuffs and a high, rounded yoke. Loose, full-length "swagger coats" followed. Coats for two- to four-year-olds had pie frills put into the waist. Fabrics were being used much more freely.

"Serve-yourself"

Teenagers in the late Forties, such as Valerie Knight (b.1931) and Bridget Hastie-Smith (b.1932), were helped to select clothes by shop assistants. The American system of "serve-yourself" did not appear in a British dress shop until 1951. The new "serve-yourself" clothes were arranged in clearly marked sizes. Customers could make a selection and then try on garments in a cubicle. It hardly sounds revolutionary now!

6 Education and Schools

Wartime damage

Education in the post-war Forties suffered from several handicaps. Wartime destruction and damage had affected about one-fifth of all educational buildings. Many other schools were in a bad state of repair as well. Normal maintenance had not been carried out during the war years because of shortages of manpower and materials.

Education Act 1944

The Education Act of 1944 made important changes. At that time, most children were attending Elementary School up to age 14. The Act ensured that nearly all children would be receiving some secondary schooling. There were to be three types of secondary schools:

"Grammar", "Technical" and "Modern". Intelligence testing at age 11 (the "11 Plus" exam) was set-up to decide which children would go to which type of school.

Hilary Strudwick (b.1939) remembers all the tension of taking the 11 Plus. "All the work in the junior top year was oriented towards getting through that exam." Those who scored highest were admitted to Grammar schools.

Another part of the 1944 Act stated that religious instruction in state schools should be made compulsory.

30 (1948) The new Bourne Secondary Modern School in Middlesex was regarded as Britain's most luxurious school.

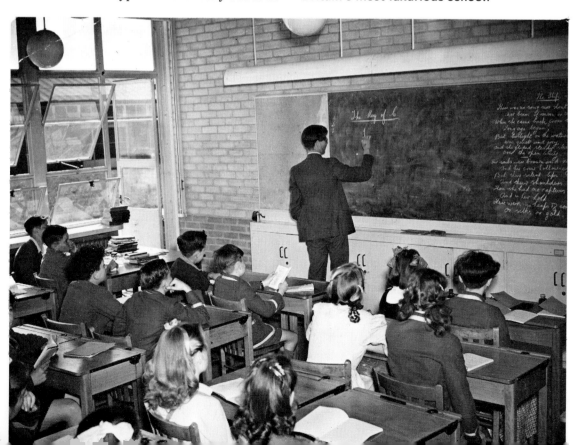

Raised school-leaving age

The school-leaving age was finally raised to 15 in 1947. (This too had been part of the 1944 Act.) "Emergency measures" were needed to cope with the extra few hundred thousand pupils staying in school. An "Emergency Training Scheme" operated from 1945 to 1949. This provided one year of intensive teacher training for over 30,000 men and women. Most of these people had been in the Forces or working in war industries. (The normal time for teachers to train was then two years.) Schools and teachers' unions were at first very doubtful about the Emergency Scheme. It turned out to be much more successful than many people had expected.

Classroom shortages

Besides more teachers, schools desperately needed more classrooms. A programme called HORSA (Hutting Operation for the Raising of the School Age) began. The huts were inadequate but necessary. About 5000 had been erected by the summer of 1948 when all 14-year-olds were at school. The HORSA huts were equipped by a programme called SFORSA (School Furniture Operation for the Raising of the School Age). The SFORSA chairs, tables, desks and stoves were all very simple in design.

Michael Taylor (b.1936) remembers the classroom shortages. "I was just in a sort of pre-fab. It wasn't a properly insulated building. We had coke stoves in the classrooms with chimneys going up through the walls."

Book shortages

In 1947, *The Times Educational Supplement* headlines talked about the "TEXT BOOK FAMINE": "The schools are using dirty and tattered copies of books which are often out of date. Children are sharing books, classes are held-up waiting for books which are in use elsewhere...." There was a shortage of over 2 million textbooks in London schools alone. The problem was nationwide but most serious in areas that had been bombed.

Children at that time did not expect much in the way of materials for learning. As Michael Storm (b.1935) recalls of Yorkshire: "We had a textbook per subject per year. We didn't have a

31 (1948) A new teaching aid called the "filmstrip" was just becoming popular. *The Times Educational Supplement* enthused about the new aid and said in 1947: "Filmstrips ready or soon to be available describe among other subjects the theatre, map-making, biology, carpentry, wood engraving, British industry one hundred years ago and coal mining."

wealth of browsing material. There was none of the endless flood of duplicated and photocopied material you have today. We had 'the book' for the year's work and that was it."

School equipment

School equipment was generally simple. Hilary Strudwick (b.1939): "Our PE in primary school was jumping on the spot and making star shapes. There were hoops, bean bags and balls but that was all the equipment. I went back to that school in the early 1950s and they had just got some wood bars and other apparatus. How envious we were."

Valerie Knight (b.1931): "There wasn't much sports equipment. Everything was very carefully given out to pupils and then handed back."

Hilary Strudwick (b.1939) was at a "Miss Crystal's" in Glasgow just after the war. The children sat at high wooden desks and used slates and chalk. She moved to Manchester in 1947 where "you didn't move about unless you were queueing up to ask the teacher a question. We had only flimsy paper to write on and we always had to use both sides." They used dip-in pens. "The wooden desks each had

32 (1950) Bicester Sunday School. Younger children sing at a special session in the "Happy Hut". Meanwhile, older children were at morning service where teams competed to see who could find various Bible verses the quickest. There were also entertainments and clubs for pupils during the week, including swimming lessons. About half of all parents were still sending children to Sunday Schools. Hilary Strudwick (b.1939): "Sunday Schools arranged a lot more things than they do now. They were very much a focus of social activities." In the late Forties regular church goers included about 11 per cent of all women and 7 per cent of men. (The overall average was about 3 per cent in the early 1980s.)

an inkwell and we had ink that was mixed from powder. It was rotten. You had to keep stirring it. Handwriting was very important. You tried to do some good writing but inevitably there were blotches with such a scratchy pen." As an older junior, she was given a fountain pen as a present. "That was great because you could fill it up with your own ink at home."

Teachers return

Teachers during the war tended to be those too

old for military and other wartime service. After the war many children suddenly found themselves with younger teachers. Michael Taylor (b.1936) remembers them coming back from the services. "The headmaster's son came back in 1948 and he arrived in uniform. The next day he was one of our masters."

Nursery/infant teacher shortages

Another problem facing education in the post-war Forties was the shortage of teachers for infant schools. The number of babies born rose each year after 1942. By 1947 these children were starting school and the demand for school places was rising sharply. A 1948 National Union of Teachers conference complained about infant classes having 40 to 50 children, with not enough space or equipment.

Children did not have much chance for nursery education in the post-war Forties. One newspaper in 1948 pointed out that Britain then had 2 million children under the age of 5. There were nursery school places for about 18,000. Make-shift classes provided some sort of schooling for only another 68,000.

33 (1949) Students of the Outward Bound School, Aberdovey, check their maps while on an expedition. The Sea School prepared males aged 16 to 20 for careers at sea. The varied curriculum also developed character and social skills.

"Travelling" children

Regular schools had problems enough coping after the war. There were also special schools with extra difficulties. A school for canal-boat children called "Cedar" was on the bank of the Grand Union Canal near Southall in London. There were about 80 children aged 5 to 15 officially on the roll, but no more than 39 ever came on one day. Sometimes there were as few as 6. Simple reading, writing and number work were all that was possible. The children missed much school but they knew all about London's canal system. Even the smallest took turns at handling the family boat or "butty". Such "travelling" children were required by law to attend school at least 200 days a year, but many did not even make this. At the Thorney Hill School in the New Forest about half the children were travellers. One ten-year-old boy there had only *ever* been to school for a life total of nine months.

"All-age" schools

There were still many "all-age" schools in the late 1940s (8,755 in England and Wales in 1947). Over a million pupils attended these with all ages from 5 to 15 together in the same building. Some were small village schools but others were in run-down inner city areas. (By the late 1960s there were only about 70 of these schools left.)

Winter of 1947

The severe winter of 1947 added to problems. Bridget Hastie-Smith (b.1932) went to a school that had been used by the services during the war. "There were still military words on the blackboards when we arrived back." The school had been damaged by bombing. "It was in an awful mess." In the very cold winter and fuel shortages of 1947 the school had no heating at all. "We still went to school. We piled on more clothes to keep warm."

Michael Storm (b.1935) and many other children did not always get to school that winter. "Over a period of three weeks there were groups of days when you physically could not get out of the village [in Yorkshire] because of the blizzards. To a child of 12 it was very exciting."

John Owen (b.1940) remembers primary school in South Wales: "The school caretaker had lots of tattoos which we associated with strength. We thought he must have been the strongest man in the world." The harsh winter of 1947 was especially memorable. It was the first time John Owen stayed at school for lunch. He remembers making "caves in the deep snow".

Teaching methods

There was much more rote learning and "learning by heart" in schools then than there is now. Hilary Strudwick (b.1939): "In junior school we had to learn psalms from the

34 (1949) Fourteen-year-old pupils at a London school made a roll-top desk using timber scrounged from many sources. Old wine boxes and part of a broken dresser were included.

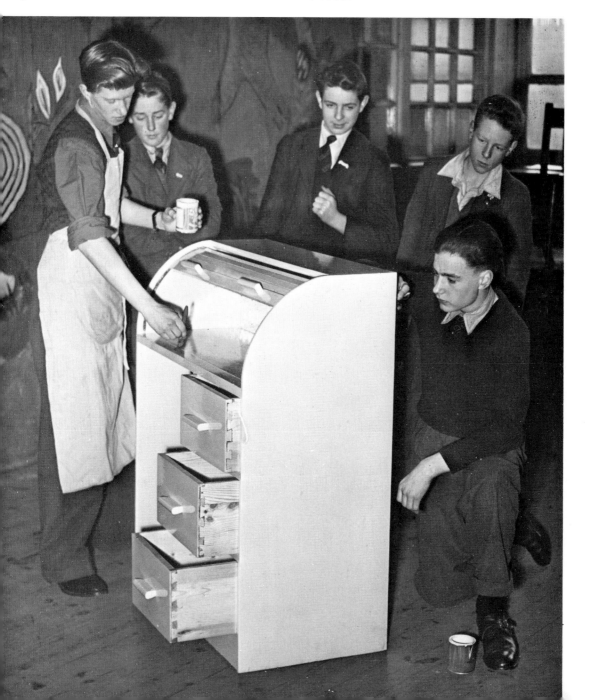

Bible by heart. 'Art' was only an occasional treat. We did cross-stitch table-mats. Nothing creative. It was a set pattern."

Michael Storm (b.1935) remembers the teaching as being very good but somewhat unimaginative: "There were only two occasions when we ever did anything outside the school. One was in Latin class when we went to look at a Roman villa. In Geography we once went up on to the school roof to get a view of the city [Hull] and the docks. We never went on any field study trips. We never talked about what was going on in the world." Examples from the recent war were sometimes brought into lessons. "The history teacher would say 'Suppose German paratroopers had landed in the park opposite. What would you have done?...'"

Schools broadcasting

Children listened to BBC schools' radio in the post-war Forties. There was a Geography series, a History series and others. A weekly 18-minute "current affairs" programme talked about something that was happening in the news. A "citizenship" series had talks by an MP, a policeman, a local councillor and others about their part in the community.

Scrapbooks and guides

In April 1946 some 30 "daily life scrapbooks" compiled by British schools were sent to America under a scheme called "Books Across the Sea". American schools sent 30 scrapbooks in return. These books described ordinary details of everyday life and were meant to help children understand the other country. Over 250 pairs of schools and clubs had already exchanged books under the scheme.

In November 1947 a group of ten-year-olds at a primary school in Enfield, Middlesex, prepared their own New Guide to Enfield. They gathered information about the houses, churches, hospitals, transport, factories and ancient buildings. Each child contributed a chapter.

35 (1949) Cookery class at a new Secondary Modern School in Stevenage. Note the style of cookers used then.

Exhibitions and visits

Also in 1947 a large exhibition was put on for parents at a school in London's East End. The school was in a side street that had suffered much bomb damage. *The Times Educational Supplement* reported: "Almost inevitably at a school exhibition these days there is a project on coal." Throughout the week children gave displays on dancing, puppetry and dramatics.

In March 1947 young people in Wembley due to leave school were paying organized visits to local factories, offices and shops. This was to help them choose future careers. Girls from Wembley Hill School were photographed looking at a shirt-drying machine during a "choose your career" visit to a local laundry.

Museums gradually re-opened after the war, with some educational programmes for children. By 1949 young people could go to London's Geffrye Museum on a Saturday and play games to help them learn history. One of these was "Happy Families" in historical costume.

Exam changes

The exam system changed as well in the late 1940s. In 1947 the Secondary School Examinations Council (SSEC) recommended to the Ministry of Education that the examinations for the School Certificate and Higher School Certificate should be replaced. These certificates were gained by passing exams in a *number* of subjects. The suggestion was for separate, single-subject examinations, *each* leading to a General Certificate of Education. An Ordinary Level was to be taken at the age of 16 and an Advanced Level was to be taken at age 18. The new GCE exams were first held in 1951.

Higher education

In the autumn of 1945 the universities were still not back to normal. Many lodgings meant for students were still housing evacuees (moved for safety during wartime). Oxford and Cambridge had only about two-thirds of the pre-war number of undergraduates in residence. The shortage of teaching staff was a big concern. During the war Oxford had run shortened, concentrated courses. These were continued in the post-war years for men back from the services.

Higher education did, however, begin to expand greatly in the post-war years. The number of university students in 1947 was already 50 per cent higher than in the autumn of 1945.

7 Books, Magazines, Newspapers

Paper shortages

Every book publisher's main problem from 1940 onwards was the shortage of raw materials, mainly paper. Shortage of paper and shortage of labour meant that many fewer books were published during the war and for some years after.

In October 1945 British publishers were being allowed collectively only 2000 tonnes of paper a month. An extra allocation of paper to publishers in February 1946 brought their paper quota to only 10 per cent of what it had been in 1939. By 1948 each publisher's paper quota was still only 85 per cent of what they had consumed pre-war. Besides the shortage of new books, over 20 million books had been destroyed by bombings in Britain during the war.

One newspaper reported in 1948 how schools were "crying out for more books". Wartime editions were worn-out and not being replaced fast enough. Many pre-war books were badly out of date. While paper was the main shortage, another problem was cloth for book covers. As the newspaper said: "All publishers of educational books have for years had a ration of paper that would be ludicrous if it were not tragic."

Michael Taylor (b.1936): "I can remember the lack of books and lack of paper at school. We were always using both sides of the paper. Notebooks were used with great care. Many of the textbooks were pre-war."

36 (1949) Books were still in short supply
Hilary Strudwick (b.1939): "We didn't have a lot of books. The ones we had we read over and over."

The shortage of paper for British publishers meant that some publishers went out of the country for printing. In January 1948 a new children's monthly magazine started called *Collin's Magazine for Boys and Girls*. This was edited in England but printed in Canada. Three-quarters of the copies went to young people in Britain. There was a serial, short stories, letters, competitions, cartoons and other illustrations.

What children read
Puffin storybooks, costing 9d (about 4 new pence) were popular gifts for Christmas 1945. (The Puffin paperbacks had only just started in 1941.) There were also many books still reflecting the recent war. *Calling All Arms* was for boys aged 12 to 16 and cost 7/6d (37½ new pence). This was illustrated, showing the manufacture and use in war of guns, tanks, aeroplanes and mines. More fanciful books included *Fluffy Duckies* for children aged five to seven, with large colour pictures of farm-yard creatures.

In December 1947 one newspaper reported: "To get one of Arthur Ransome's children's books for Christmas is to be in luck. Booksellers are said to keep copies of Ransome's books hidden away for favourite customers. That is the height of literary fame and favour these days – that your books should share an under-the-counter status with a rabbit, an ox-tail or a bit of offal."

A questionnaire about books was given to over a hundred 12- to 14-year-olds in Liverpool in 1947. The favourite type of book cited was "school stories". Simple Arthur Ransome-type adventure stories were next in popularity. Discovery and exploration came third, with historical novels fourth. Authors who appealed most were W. E. Johns, Angela Brazil, P. F. Westerman and Enid Blyton. Some children also mentioned Robert Louis Stevenson, Charles Dickens, H. G. Wells, John Buchan and Lewis Carroll.

In 1949 there was a new and attractive series of travel letters called *My Foreign Correspondent*. Over 2500 schools subscribed to these.

Many parents gave sets as presents to their children. The letters had all sorts of information about life in foreign countries.

Lending libraries
Valerie Knight (b.1931) began working as a librarian in 1948. She recalls how "books were issued for one week or two. The one-week 'Class A' books were the newer ones. After six months they reverted to normal stock". The scarcity of books meant that overdue volumes were certainly missed. Valerie Knight: "We went out to retrieve overdue books. This was one of the least favourite jobs. There were hazards to combat like fierce dogs and furious people."

Libraries were so short of books that an experiment was tried in early 1948. Outside each public library in Greater London was put a large box with a slot in the lid. These were used to receive books that had been borrowed during the war and had not been brought back. Hundreds of volumes, some overdue by four and more years, were anonymously returned.

Besides public libraries, in the late 1940s books were lent out for a penny or two a week from some chain stores and small shops. Paperbacks had started in the 1930s but were not nearly as plentiful as they are now.

Key novels
A favourite novel of the time was Graham Greene's *The Heart of the Matter,* published in 1948. This story took place in a West African colony as British colonialism was ending. Another novel reflecting post-war Britain was George Orwell's *Nineteen Eighty Four,* published in 1949. This showed a grim view of society at a time when the worry about fascist dictatorship was recent indeed.

Magazines and newspapers
Periodicals faced paper shortages as well. In May 1947 newspapers and magazines were still limited to one-quarter of the amount of paper they had before the war. By 1949 the amount of newsprint being imported was still only one-third of pre-war supplies.

Picturegoer was one popular magazine. Bridget Hastie-Smith (b.1932) used to cut out photos of her favourite films and film stars. "My greatest loves at the time were James Mason and Stewart Granger." (Some other big stars were Ronald Colman, Loretta Young, Fredric March and Olivia de Havilland.)

37 (1950) A new children's comic called the *Eagle* was launched. Philip Heater, aged nine, compared this to the American comics popular in Britain at the time: *"Eagle* is jolly good. Mostly it's adventure strips and serials."

8 Work and Industry

Choice of jobs

The first post-war "Schoolboys' Exhibition" was held at Westminster Central Hall in December 1946. (Pre-war exhibitions dated back to 1927.) Displays included one by Cable and Wireless Ltd where boys could actually send telegrams to one another. There was a life-sized model of the driver's cabin of an Underground Train. The stands related to popular hobbies, and, more importantly, to future jobs. People working in various occupations were there to talk to boys and advise.

The choice of jobs for young people starting work was somewhat different in the late Forties from the choice today. There were many more jobs in agriculture, forestry and fishing as well as in mining and quarrying, textiles, clothing and as domestic servants. There were many fewer jobs in the public sector working for central government and local authorities. There were many fewer jobs in "service" industries generally.

Percentage of UK labour force in :	% 1949	% 1980
agriculture	10	2
industry	47	42
services	43	56

The kinds of industries open to young people changed significantly after the war. Industries were developing around such products as plastics, synthetic fibres and fertilizers. Two new science-based industries were electronics and optics. Engineering was expanding greatly.

National Service

There was less choice than today with regard to military service. The National Service Act

38 (1948) A linen mill in Northern Ireland. The barefoot 14-year-old on the left is called a "doffer", changing bobbins on the spinning frame for about £2 a week. The mills were working at about 20 per cent below capacity because of shortage of workers and other difficulties. Wartime regulations had allowed children under 16 to work as long as 48 hours a week in textile factories. This expired in 1946. The Minister of Labour was then urged by factories to continue these extended hours but this was refused.

of 1948 required 18-year-old males (about 160,000 young men each year) to report for a compulsory two-year period of military service. (This "National Service" was abolished in 1960.) A 1949 opinion poll showed half of those interviewed wanting conscription to continue in peacetime. One-third wanted it to end. Bridget Hastie-Smith (b.1932): "The boys disappeared at the age of 18 for two years and came back as young men."

Nationalization

The new Labour government elected after the war much extended public ownership of industry. A series of Nationalization Acts were passed. In 1946 nationalization included the Bank of England, the Coal Industry and

39 (1947) Thirteen boys aged 14 to 16 built homes on an estate at Addington, Surrey. They were supervised by a master bricklayer and carpenter. Bricks, wood and other materials were still in short supply.

Civil Aviation. In 1947 the electricity industry became state-owned. The railways and gas industry were nationalized in 1948 with the iron and steel industries added in 1949. There had been some government ownership of industry before the war (for example, the BBC, the Post Office and the British Overseas Airways Corporation). Post-war Nationalization Acts included a much greater part of industry in Britain than ever before.

"Reports to the Nation"

Growing government involvement in industry included "Report to the Nation" boxes published in newspapers. These were intended to encourage people to work harder and produce more. In May 1948 the "Report to the Nation No. 17" said: "This is the most critical year since the war. Our very life as a nation depends on a rising tide of production...." "Report to the Nation No. 18" in June was headed "The Nation's Credit Column". This highlighted examples of people whose hard work was helping Britain. There was a picture of Peggy Mayor, aged 17, who worked for a firm in Preston. She was "responsible for an average production of 113,000 yards of 'weft' a week which goes to making 12,838 typewriter ribbons – a most valuable export". The praise of Peggy was meant to encourage others. "We are 48 million people struggling to earn a living in our small island....What are you doing to qualify for Credit Column? It still adds up to more and more production...."

"Report to the Nation No. 22" in August 1948 was titled "Britain Waking Up": "You'd be surprised how much ground British industries are breaking these days. Many are doing a great service by producing goods we used to import. But we are still importing 23/7d worth of goods for every 20/- worth we export.There is an urgent need for more enterprise, efficiency and effort."

Shortage of labour

Part of the crisis facing Britain was a shortage of workers. Companies were desperately competing with one another to attract young people. Employers went out to schools and youth clubs to try to make their own trade sound most appealing. The firms that had the most difficulty in holding employees were those with poor facilities. Many workrooms were dreary and lacked even basic staff provisions such as a canteen.

The raising of the school leaving age in 1947 meant fewer young people coming out of school into work. This was at a time when labour was already short. The loss of juvenile labour was about 130,000 in September 1947 and up to 380,000 by December 1948. The new law required young people of 14 to stay at school until age 15. Young people of 14 had been out working doing all sorts of jobs, including messenger work, work as van boys and minor clerical jobs. As one newspaper warned when the leaving age was raised: "Over the next 18 months industry and agriculture will have to make some major adjustments."

The shortage of labour meant a low level of unemployment. In fact unemployment was at a fairly low level for nearly 25 years after the war. Under 2 per cent unemployed was the average. Unemployment temporarily rose to about 3 per cent in 1947. This was because of the great freeze-up, with blizzards followed by floods. Many factories had to shut temporarily because of the fuel shortage and other difficulties.

Women at work

As well as trying to attract young people, industries were trying to bring more women back to work. Many women who had been obliged to work during the war left their

40 (1949) Nearly 2000 hop-pickers arrived at Buston Manor near Maidstone, Kent. Picking hops was a working holiday for many East End children. Beds were made by packing clean straw into covers to make mattresses.

factory jobs as soon as they could. Day nurseries which had looked after young children during the war were afterwards no longer being supported by central government. The cost was put back on to local authorities who shut many nurseries as an economy measure. As a result, women with young children found it much more difficult to work in industry.

Women were also resenting the poor conditions of many factories and their low rates of pay. A female journalist in one 1946 newspaper said: "Two questions are uppermost in women's minds at the moment, the first that of equal pay for equal work, the second being the chances of equal opportunity." A new book in 1946 called *The Rate for the Job* emphasized that housewives should be seen as "working" women as well. These early stirrings of "Women's Liberation" in the late 1940s grew stronger over the following decades. The percentage of married women in the labour force was much lower in the post-war Forties than in the 1980s. Only about 20 per cent of married women were in paid work, compared to over 50 per cent by the 1980s.

41 **(1948) William Robertson, age 11, helped to harvest oats. Young people were still needed for farm jobs as labour was so short.**

Children in farming

Shortages of labour meant that even children were needed to help with farming. A number of "harvest camps" were set up in 1946. Each usually had about 30 campers, two masters, one or two cooks and two or three camp orderlies. Rural schools and village halls were used for sleeping. Harvest campers were given cheap fares to travel by train to where they were helping. A joint message was sent to schools in May 1947 from the Minister of Agriculture and the Minister of Education. At least 50,000 boys and girls were needed to help on the land that summer, as well as the help needed from children during term-time. The main need during term-time was for help with potato planting and lifting.

Michael Taylor (b.1936) remembers helping with fruit picking. "A gang of us went from school and there were a lot of other youngsters as well. We slept in some sort of barn. It was tremendous fun but precious little fruit picking got done. We were eating fruit all the time. I remember sitting in a cherry tree for a couple of days and just eating. Marvellous!"

In March, 1949 a Norfolk MP spoke in the House of Commons about growing opposition to the continued use of schoolchildren in farming. Local education authorities objected especially. The MP asked for a guarantee that this was the last year that children would be used. The Minister of Education replied that he could not give such a guarantee. There was still a great shortage of labour for farming tasks.

Gypsy children

Children also assisted their parents in various trades and helped with light jobs. A newspaper photo in December 1948 showed gypsy children in Buckinghamshire making Christmas decorations for sale. This was a traditional trade for gypsies (who preferred the names "travellers", "showmen" or "vanners"). To make the artificial flowers the children needed only a jack-knife, dye, string, a little wood and some crab-apples which they collected in the thicket.

"My first job"

The experience of starting work was somewhat different for young people in the post-war Forties. Shortages of labour meant that jobs were certainly easier to find than in the 1980s . Valerie Knight (b.1931) recalls the first day of her first job, in a public library. It was 18 August 1948: "I reported for duty wearing the only outfit I had that wasn't school uniform (a green hand-knitted jumper with a grey pleated skirt). I had cycled, and my curled hair was quite straight from the damp air. The front door of the building wasn't yet open. I decided to reconnoitre the back and was met by a bewildering number of gates and doors. I pushed my bike through one and was received into the back of an establishment that proved to be Boots the Chemists. They were also expecting a new junior library assistant as the shop had a lending library in those days. It was some time before the confusion was cleared up...."

Fuel shortages in the late 1940s meant electricity cuts in public places and businesses as well as at home. Valerie Knight remembers what happened in the library: "We had all these hurricane lamps and candles. You'd know the lights were going off at certain times and you'd have the lamps ready. We used to get all the people out and we'd wait for the lights to come on again."

Valerie Knight also recalls how much more formal work was. "We were all 'Miss' and 'Mister'. Christian names could be used only behind the scenes. There was a great division between senior and junior staff and a rigid demarcation of duties. You never questioned what you were told to do. There were quite strict rules about what you wore and if what you wore was thought unsuitable you could be sent home to change. If you were unlucky you would receive a stern lecture from the Chief Librarian ending in the words 'young lady'."

42 (1947) Members of the Enfield Boys' Brigade took on the job of repairing toddlers' toys for Enfield's day nurseries. Valerie Knight (b.1931): "Things had to last. You had to look after things. It's much more a throw-away society now than it was in those days."

9 Transport

Railways, trolleybuses and trams

Millions of pounds of damage had been done to Britain's railways during the war. This made post-war travelling that much more difficult. People then relied on public road and rail transport (steam trains) more than in the 1980s.

Hilary Strudwick (b.1939) recalls the trams in Glasgow just after the war: "They always seemed so high to get on to." Michael Taylor (b.1936) came up to London from Surrey by tram: "When the trams reached the terminus all the seats had to be pushed over the other way so passengers on the return journey would be facing forward. The cars themselves were not turned around."

There were trolleybuses near Hilary Strudwick's grandparents in Yorkshire: "These were driven by electricity. They gave a very smooth and quiet ride compared with trams and buses." In the late Forties buses were just beginning to take over from the trolleybuses and trams in towns.

Private cars

The great increase in private car ownership was only just starting by 1948. There were then just two million private cars and vans on the road. Road surfaces were still rough in many places. The first motorway was not even announced until 1955. An important trend since the late Forties has been much more use of aeroplanes and private cars and relatively less reliance on rail and public road services.

Petrol was rationed during the war and up to 1950. This also made travelling more difficult. The ration did increase by 50 per cent in 1946. In the severe winter of 1947 the shortage of fuel caused much transport to stop altogether. Britain also then had its worst floods for fifty years. Many roads were im-

43 (1947) A boy checks the London Underground station map, as it looked then. With many fewer private cars, people then depended much more on public transport than they do today.

passable. Children watched as workmen and prisoners of war were busy trying to clear paths.

Buying a private car after the war was made harder because of low production. One newspaper reported in early 1946 that the "main question being asked by motorists today is 'How can I get a new car? Where? When?'" Shortages of labour and of certain materials held up car manufacture along with nearly everything else.

Derek Walker (b.1934) recalls his school friends in Northern Ireland wearing badges with the symbols of motor car companies. "People used to swap the badges. There were nearly all British cars on the roads then. Austins, Rovers...."

Cycling

Cycling was generally safer in the late Forties than now because traffic was so much lighter. Michael Taylor (b.1936) remembers the sort of freedom children had on their bikes: "I used to cycle to school, seven miles to and seven miles

44 (1946) A picnic cup of tea. Petrol was still rationed and private motoring much less common than it is today.

back. You wouldn't allow a ten-year-old to cycle on those main roads now because the traffic is so heavy." Michael and his brother used to cycle 65 miles down to visit their grandfather in Sussex. "Our mother knew that we would take all day to get there. We'd stay with him for two or three days and then we'd cycle home again. Imagine allowing a 14- and 12-year-old to do that now over those busy roads."

When Michael Taylor left his bicycle it was never locked. "You used to just stick your bicycle by some railings and come back for it later."

Street lighting

Bicycles were used for work as well as play. Bridget Hastie-Smith (b.1932) recalls the evening street lamplighter. "He came along and put up his long stick, clicking the street

51

light on. He was so skilled he wouldn't even come off his bicycle." Hilary Strudwick (b.1939) was in Glasgow just after the war. The lamplighter on her street came on foot. (Many children saw street lighting for the first time after the war. During the war streets had been blacked-out to avoid helping enemy bombers.)

Horse-drawn vans

Horse-drawn carts were still used for deliveries in some areas in the post-war Forties.

Michael Taylor (b.1936) remembers milk arriving this way. Vans delivering bread in Northern Ireland were also drawn by horses. Derek Walker (b.1934): "Delivery men knocked at the door. They stopped and chatted and sometimes they came in for a cup of tea."

Horses on the streets meant that natural "droppings" were left. These were gathered eagerly by householders to fertilize their gardens. Many late Forties' children helped to collect this valuable manure.

10 Holidays, Sports, Entertainments

Holidays away

All the difficulties of travelling in the late Forties meant that many children never had holidays away. A 1948 survey by the British Tourist Holiday Board showed that only half the British population spent its holiday away from home. A further 9 per cent had occasional day-trips. 41 per cent did not go away from home for a holiday at all.

Some lucky children left London in August 1946 for Weston-super-Mare on a "Kiddies' Express" train. There were entertainers on board. A parade of carts, donkeys and ponies greeted the children as they arrived. Youngsters rode in an open car with "Princess Elizabeth" gaily lettered on the side.

Bridget Hastie-Smith (b.1932) had a holiday away in 1947, the first her family had taken since 1939. They went to Cornwall by car and needed to save up petrol coupons for the journey. For Valerie Knight (b.1931) a family holiday in 1946 made a great impression: "We went to Jersey which the Germans had occupied during the war. People there had been shocked by the experience. There were still all the pillboxes on the beach." (Pillboxes were small concrete shelters, each holding a gun platform.)

A holiday taken by Michael Taylor (b.1936) as late as 1949 still reminded all the family of

45 **(1948) Wakefield authority built and furnished a school at Hornsea-on-Sea. For 30 shillings (£1.50) children could enjoy a three-week stay. They had lessons at the school and also time to enjoy the seaside.**

46 (1949) Children and adults enjoy a Punch-and-Judy show on the beach at Margate.

the war. The Taylors took their car on a ferry to Dunkirk, still a wrecked area. The drive to Switzerland then took about three days. "The roads nearly knocked the car to pieces. On at least one occasion we came to a bombed out bridge and had to travel to the next bridge to get across. France was a wrecked country. That was a very dramatic holiday. It made a very big impression on me. It was so much worse than conditions in Britain."

In 1948 "Bevin Boys" and factory hands between the ages of 15 and 18 had the chance for a holiday at Ambleside in the Lake District. They paid just three pounds and ten shillings a week for their keep and such activities as boating. ("Bevin Boys" referred to those 10 per cent of boys reaching military service age who were required to work in the mines. Ernest Bevin, Minister of Labour, had begun this scheme in 1943 because of the shortage of miners.)

Outings

Some outings that had not been possible during wartime were enjoyed by children again after the war. Tower Beach, near Tower Bridge in London, was closed in 1939 but re-opened in 1946 and was very popular. East End children welcomed the chance to paddle, splash and build sand castles once again.

In late 1945 children still could not visit the Science Museum in London as this had not yet re-opened. Because of wartime damage, London's Natural History Museum and the British Museum were also still closed. The Tower of London did not re-open until January 1946.

Michael Taylor (b.1936) remembers much more community activity in those days compared with now: "I can recall great big picnic parties. We used to go off on our bikes. About seven or eight families would get together and ride off on to the North Downs for a picnic and rounders and cricket."

Bridget Hastie-Smith (b.1932): "One enjoyed very simple things then. I can remember going out bluebelling on my bicycle. Carpets of bluebells. We used to bring flowers home and put them in vases. The roads were much emptier. It was much safer on your bicycle."

Sports and hobbies

People desperately wanted to enjoy themselves after six years of war. Leisure activities boomed in centres such as Blackpool and Scarborough. Once again there were large crowds for football.

Michael Storm (b.1935) recalls cricket re-turning for the first county season in 1946. "I didn't know anything about the game. There was a team from India which, at the time, meant the whole of the sub-continent." (The partition into India and Pakistan did not happen until 1947.)

Some sports events used homemade equipment. There were carts made from wooden soapboxes on pram wheels. Races were called "packing case derbies". Another popular activity was Saturday morning ice skating at a local rink.

Collecting was, as always, a favourite children's pastime. Michael Storm (b.1935) was one of many children who enjoyed stamps. "I remember the Royal Tour of South Africa in 1947 partly because I was quite a keen collector and all those special stamps were issued then."

47 (1947) A cycle-racing track was cleared amidst the bomb rubble in New Cross, London. Hilary Strudwick (b.1939) recalls the bomb craters on land near their home in Manchester. "They provided a very good cycling track with lots of ups and downs right through the bottom where the bomb fell."

55

Youth centres

Youth centres were opened to try to keep children from playing on the dirty and sometimes dangerous bomb sites. The Rodney Youth Centre in Liverpool charged two (large, old) pennies as an entrance fee in 1949. This was not paid by the poorest children. There were hobbies classes, arts and crafts, as well as a gym. Here children could push scooters, roll tyres, fight, and generally rough and tumble in greater safety than on the streets. A large bell was rung at closing time.

Scouting and clubs

Scouting continued to attract young people in the post-war Forties. Boy Scout membership in 1949 was over 470,000, the highest yet. In the summer of 1947 the Sixth World Jamboree of Boy Scouts was held in France. This was called "the Jamboree of Peace" and included scouts from over 50 countries, including Britain. Fine weather blessed the summer of 1947 and about 170 British boy scout groups

camped with partner groups in European countries. Many groups from Europe came to camp in Britain. The 1946 annual report of the Girl Guides Association described how in that year many guides from Europe visited the UK. There were also two successful international camps.

Young Farmers Clubs were popular. At the end of 1946 there were over 1200 clubs with over 65,000 members. In 1949 over 200,000 boys belonged to the National Association of Boys' Clubs. There was also a National Association of Girls' Clubs and Mixed Clubs with over 166,000 members in over 2000 clubs.

Music and dancing

Dance halls were very popular with those of teen age. A rule sometimes posted in these was "NO JIVING". The expression "teenager" was only just coming into use, having been brought from America during the war. The British teenager in the late 1940s had not yet become a recognized force in society. This happened after 1950.

Bridget Hastie-Smith (b.1932) enjoyed going to dances. "Latin American music was very

48 (1946) Acton Sports Club. Weight-lifting was a popular activity.

49 (1949) A boy scout taking a neighbour's children for a walk. A "Bob-a-job" week was held in April. Every scout was asked to earn at least one shilling towards central headquarters' administration costs by doing odd jobs. Scouts did such jobs as shopping and shining shoes. (In "Scout Job Week" of the 1980s, all the money raised is kept by each group.) A new beret was introduced in 1949 for boys over 15 to wear informally. However, the wide-brimmed hat was still part of the standard uniform. Michael Taylor (b.1936): "There was no starch. We used to put some sugar in water, soak the hat brim in that, and then iron. This kept the brims looking stiff and smart."

popular. We used to do sambas and rumbas." She remembers watching the new fast jiving. "I was fascinated." At home she had 78 rpm records and a wind-up gramophone. "It was very noisy. You had to rush to wind it up some more when you heard it winding down."

Music and other arts generally received a boost after the war. The Wartime Council for the Encouragement of Music and the Arts was changed in 1946 into the Arts Council. A Local Government Act of 1948 allowed local authorities to raise up to sixpence on the rates for the support of arts activities.

Films

Mass entertainment was still dominated by the cinema. Ever-popular throughout the war, films remained a great escape from the drabness of life in post-war years. In 1946 one-third of the UK population was going to the cinema once a week and 13 per cent were going as often as twice.

Films with a "U" certificate were judged to be suitable for everyone. Films labelled "A" were more suitable for adults. A few films were "H" (for "horrific"). The "H" was ended in 1951 and replaced by the "X". Only those over the age of 16 were allowed into "X" films. The "X" certificate marked the start of excluding children from some films. (Before 1951, the only restriction was that sometimes children had to be accompanied by an adult.)

Most films were American. Payments to Hollywood were huge, totalling about 70 million dollars a year by 1947. As Britain was in such economic crisis, the Chancellor of the Exchequer in August 1947 imposed a customs

50 (1949) A youth centre dance in Liverpool. Hit tunes of the year had titles like "Cruising Down the River" and "Powder Your Face with Sunshine".

duty on imported films. This was to stop so much money leaving the country. America's Motion Picture Association was angry and suspended all shipments of films to England.

The cut-off from America increased pressure to produce more films in Britain. Rank was the big film man of the day, controlling most of production and much of distribution. In the rush, some British films of both poor and brilliant quality were made. Among the best were the 1949 Ealing Studios comedies *Passport to Pimlico, Whiskey Galore,* and *Kind Hearts and Coronets.*

Pupils at Pendragon Hall, Reading were great film fans and made their own productions as well. The headmaster operated the camera. In summer 1947 they made a single-reel silent film called *The Nine Bright Shiners or Shocking Robbery at Bishops Bedsocks.* Parents and children visiting the school fête acted as extras for crowd scenes.

There was a definite shortage of good films for children in the post-war Forties. The

51. (1950) Young people practising in a Bicester "Red Rhythmics" Band. The instruments included harmonicas and accordian. Hilary Strudwick (b.1939): "There was a lot more making our own entertainment."

National Under Fourteens Council published a report in June 1947 called "Those Saturday Morning Cinema Clubs". This report had investigated 19 clubs in London in 1946. About a thousand children aged three to fourteen went to these. The report thought the clubs very unruly: "The manager makes various announcements which are listened to by a few amid the cries and calls and whistles of the many. Because so many of the films shown do not hold their interest, the children talk and shout and move about." Club sponsors agreed about the shortage of suitable films.

UK children did see the Pathé news-shorts at the cinema. These showed world events in the news, including all the hardships still being faced on the Continent. Michael Taylor (b.1935): " It all seemed so far away." In 1948 the United Nations estimated that in Europe alone there were 35 to 40 million children in extreme need of food and clothing.

Radio

Radio was the main source of news and entertainment in the home. Hilary Strudwick (b.1939): "Listening to the radio was much more important than it is now." In 1946 Britain had over 10.5 million receiving sets, the second largest number of any country in the world.

(The USA with over 60 million sets had nearly half of the world's total.)

Reorganization at the end of the war produced three separate radio services. "The Light Programme" was aimed at mainly a working-class audience. "The Home Service Programme" was aimed at mainly the middle-classes. "The Third Programme" was meant to appeal to upper-middle and upper classes.

A radio highlight was "The Children's Hour" which ran for 55 minutes each day at five o'clock. Features included talks, music and outside recordings. "Children's Hour Request Weeks" were started again after a lapse of six years of war.

For Michael Taylor (b.1936) the favourite was "Dick Barton Special Agent" which ran for a quarter of an hour most evenings. "He was a Private Eye who was always getting into frightfully dangerous situations. The quarter

52 (1948) Two boys are amazed at the marvel of television. Many children did not see television until after 1950. Sets were still not widely owned in the post-war Forties.

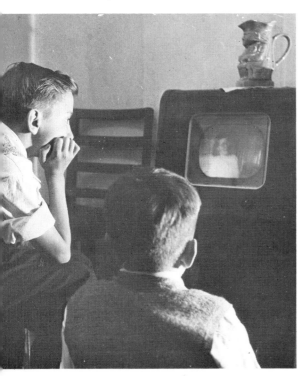

of an hour would end with him dangling with one finger from the hour hand of Big Ben or something like that. I tried never to miss an episode." Derek Walker (b.1934): "My friends and I used to re-enact Dick Barton."

Television
Television had only just started in the late 1930s and was shut down for the duration of war. Services were resumed on 7 June 1946 but grew only slowly. There were at first only two sessions of television daily: 3:00 p.m. to 4:30 p.m. and then 8:00 p.m. to 10:00 p.m. Licences bought in 1947 numbered fewer than 14,000 but by 1951 there were well over 700,000 licence-holders.

At first, television could be seen only by those in an area of 30 miles around London (because of limited transmitter power). By 1949, television could be seen also in the Midlands. (It was 1953 before most of the country was covered.)

In 1948 a Sunday afternoon hour "For the Children" began. This was the first children's programme on British television and used a troupe of puppets, including "Muffin the Mule". Cameras sometimes showed children in the studio audience with rapt concentration on their faces.

John Owen (b.1940) remembers seeing television for the first time when he was about ten years old. Screens were very small and there was no colour. Michael Taylor (b.1936): "The first time I saw television was the boat-race in 1950. I went to a friend's house and I couldn't have been more disappointed. The picture was so bad you could hardly see anything."

Parties
Parties were a more familiar entertainment for children. War "victory" parties continued well after V-E and V-J Day celebrations in the middle of 1945. In early January 1946 Ebbw Vale workers of the Richard Thomas steel plant in Wales gave probably the largest victory party in the country. Over 3000 children from surrounding districts were brought to the steel works. One of the large

inspection rooms was converted for the occasion. "Santa Claus" drove round the tables in a sledge drawn by a swan built round a tractor. On their way to the party some children stopped and watched molten steel being taken from furnaces.

Halloween parties were important to children in Northern Ireland, Scotland and the north of England. Derek Walker (b.1934)

53 (1946) Two boys play in the band at the Grasmere and Lake District Annual Athletic Sports. This was being held for the first time since 1939. Because of the war, many events and recreations were cancelled for years. The post-war Forties was a time for reviving such traditions.

recalls that in Northern Ireland items would be baked in apple tarts. "People put in rings, sixpences, mottoes....Whoever got the ring was supposed to get married. The sixpence stood for wealth. If you got a tiny bit of dishcloth in your tart it meant you were going to do the washing-up for the year."

Christmas

The most universal celebration was, of course, Christmas. For the holidays in 1945 there were still restrictions left over from the war. For example, the Ministry of Fuel and Power ruled: "No outdoor display or lighting" as a way to save fuel. There were, however, two pantomimes showing in London's West End (*Aladdin* and *Cinderella*) and a variety of Christmas plays.

"The Children's Hour" radio programme broadcast the story *A Room at the Inn* on Christmas Eve 1945. On Christmas Day there was a radio exchange of carols and greetings amongst children of various countries. There was also a "Christmas Regional Round" with teasers and quizzes put to boys and girls all over Britain.

Christmas gradually became better but remnants of war left their mark for years. In 1947 one newspaper commented: "Christmas is not what it was, so many will say with a sigh. In this time of shortages and restrictions with, for most, no turkey on the table and less travelling to share the festival with friends, there is much to complain of."

By Christmas 1948 there was a return to crackers and Christmas tree decorations, but the need to save fuel continued. Shop exteriors were still not lit up after dark.

Michael Taylor (b.1936): "Presents were often second-hand things that had been gleaned here and there." Bridget Hastie-Smith (b.1932): "We had this squirrel-like approach to things. You kept your wrapping paper from one year to the next."

By Christmas 1949 things *were* very much better. The new novelty song sung loudly by children was "Rudolph the Red-Nosed Reindeer".

11 Toys and Games

Shortage of toys

Supplies of toys, like nearly everything else, were affected by the war. A newspaper report in November 1945 commented on the shortage of toys for Christmas. Some things, like children's swings and mechanical toys that had not been seen for years were then back in stock. Plastic dolls were available but very few dolls' prams. Only about one-sixth of the demand for children's tricycles could be met. The greatest favourite with boys was a model RAF helicopter kit. There were wooden chessmen carved from old police truncheons. Clockwork toys were popular but these disappeared quickly once in the shops. The newspaper quoted one salesman as saying: "We get in a hundred in the morning and the shoppers come in like a horde of locusts and the counter is cleared."

Michael Storm (b.1935) remembers having an almost physical craving for toys: "Boys a fraction older than me did have soldiers, little farm animals, toy guns, that sort of thing. I had this tremendous envy. I didn't really have any toys. That was partly our shortage of money also there just weren't many in the shops." He recalls doing a "terrible thing" after the war. "We had very little money because my mother was a war widow. I used to go down every Saturday to the village shop. Once when I was there on a little shelf in the corner were the first Dinky toys I'd seen. (Small, model "Dinky Toys" had begun in 1933.) There was just a small selection of military vehicles – little search-light carriers, armoured cars. I was totally fascinated by these. On a mad impulse I asked the village shopkeeper for one of those

54 (1948) Dolls were as popular as ever. Hilary Strudwick (b.1939): "I remember with particular affection one celluloid doll, Angela, who had her head broken by being dropped. She was all done up with plaster because there was no way you could repair it."

55 (1946) The new small novelty toy for Christmas was the "Wakouwa". It could be made to move by pressing the bottom of the base.

and one of those. [He added on the cost to the family's outstanding account.] Of course they were terribly expensive. This caused a terrific upset at home because my mother just couldn't afford to pay for them."

Gerald Pudney (b.1944) had his Dinky toys lined up "on a rack with narrow shelves which my Dad had made". His father also made a marble alley out of bits of wood. "I had a vast collection of marbles."

Slowly, factories returned to producing toys. One huge factory in Erith, Kent, that made guns during the war, was turning out thousands of toys a week by 1947. These included "Roll-a-bye" roller skates, "ideal for beginners".

Materials for toys
Plastics and other synthetics became much more widely used for toys after the war. In 1948 a mother wrote to a manufacturer complaining of those "darn plastic" toys which are "beautiful to look at but rarely last two days".

Traditional materials such as wood were still used as well. A popular toy for Christmas 1949 was puppet dolls for a play, sold with gramophone records. The wooden-jointed "actors" could be made to dance to the music.

Shortage of safe play-space
Besides the shortage of toys, there was also a shortage of safe places for children to play. A newspaper reported in 1947 on the lack of leisure-time facilities for children out of school. Housing was so cramped that many under-14-year-olds were out on the streets until late every night because they had nowhere else to play. Play centres that were available were usually overcrowded and suitable only for those under age 11. The National Under Fourteens Council set out to press local authorities to provide more leisure-time facilities. The Council also trained men and women willing to help as volunteers.

Street games
Hilary Strudwick (b.1939) remembers playing far more street games than is possible in cities now. She lived in Manchester and cars were relatively few in her area. From the ages of about seven to nine she played several games

62

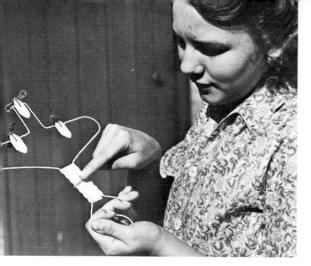

56 (1947) Skeleton aeroplanes were a popular toy. Rubbing the serrations with a piece of wire set up vibrations which caused the three propellors to revolve. Shortages of nearly everything meant that toys were made using as little materials as possible.

57 (1950) A popular street game was "Weak 'orses, Weak 'orses" to the cries of "Jimmy Jimmy Knacker 1,2,3, Jimmy Jimmy Knacker 1,2,3,...". It was rather rough and banned by some schools.

where one person who was "on" stood at one side of the road. Everyone else stood on the other side and competed to be the first across. For example, in "Letters in Your Name", the person who was "on" would call out a letter. "You took a step forward for each time that letter appeared in your name. If 'E' were called out and you had three 'Es' in your name, you took three steps. Then another letter would be called. The first person to reach the other side of the road became 'on'. You couldn't play that nowadays, with the traffic." Another similar game involved calling out the initials of film stars. "We didn't have television so the cinema was much more important." The person who was "on" called out two initials. If you thought you knew which film star these stood for you rushed across the road. The first person to tag the other side and say the right name (say, "Betty Grable" for "BG" or "Bob Hope" for "BH") became "on". Then they could call out two initials.

Imaginative games

Hilary Strudwick (b.1939): "We made up a lot more imaginative games. I used to play 'school' with flat, two-dimensional paper dolls. These came back in a few years after the war and were very popular. I used to have a far bigger collection than anything I've seen nowadays." Hilary Strudwick also recalls the little coloured motifs called "scraps". "You could buy different figures. I played all sorts of imaginative games with those. There were different sheets, say, on 'occupations' showing a baker, chimney sweep...."

58 (1950) Hop-scotch and skipping were favourite games with girls. Hilary Strudwick (b.1939): "We definitely played out a lot more than kids today. You would go to 'play out'."

12 Crime and Mischief

Juvenile crime

Increasing crime was a worry in the post-war Forties. In late 1945 the Secretary of State for the Home Department commented on why he thought this a growing issue: "Crime is one of the inevitable hangovers of war. For six years the world has abandoned the rule of law. Temptations have been constantly multiplying. Things which were abundant in 1938 are now as rare as gold dust and therefore infinitely desirable. No one would have thought of stealing a second-hand shirt in 1938. Today the sight of a shirt on a clothes line has become a temptation. Everything is worth stealing and everything is much easier to steal. Any amateur can get into a bombed house which has still got its windows boarded up with cardboard."

By 1948 the number of young people convicted of breaking the law was still rising sharply. There were twice as many boys and girls in prison in 1948 as in 1938. A Criminal Justice Act passed in 1948 restricted sentences of imprisonment on youthful offenders. The system of probation was extended and new detention centres were established for offenders aged 14 to 21.

In early 1949 there was a conference in

59 (1946) Playing on a bomb site in London's East End. The disruption of war meant not enough safe play areas. There were fewer general facilities for recreation. This was partly to blame for the sharp rise in crime and mischief by young people.

London on the whole problem of juvenile delinquency. It was felt that more playing fields and clubs would provide lawful outlets for youthful energy. The number of playing fields in 1949 was still much fewer than before the war. In London, the number of cricket pitches in parks and open spaces had fallen from 350 pre-war to only 80 by the late Forties. The number of football pitches was down from 436 to 150.

Familiar mischief

One bit of mischief as common in the late Forties as ever was stealing apples from orchards. Called "scrumping" by some, the term for this varied around Britain. Derek Walker (b.1934): "In Northern Ireland we called this 'fogging' an orchard."

Halloween was a time for tricks and pranks in Northern Ireland, as well as Scotland and the north of England. In the rest of England, "Mischief Night" before the fifth of November was more important. Hilary Strudwick (b.1939): "It was usual to take gates off hinges or throw fireworks into gardens. Some of the boys took that a bit far and put fireworks through letterboxes. People who were crotchety about letting you get your ball out of their garden would prepare for this by putting a bucket of water inside under the letterbox." Hilary Strudwick also remembers other standard mischief such as "tying cotton to the door knocker and hiding behind the wall. You knocked at the door so people came out and nobody was there."

13 The Festival Year

Morrison's "Folly"?

In December 1947 Minister Herbert Morrison announced in the House of Commons the idea of a national exhibition for 1951. There was

60 (1951) A family rests by a fountain at the "Festival of Britain". The exhibition was welcome after so many years of hardship. A new decade and easier times began.

general support for the project as a boost for the nation's morale. However, Britain's economic situation was still bleak. The UK was at the time still spending the last of its American loan. By early 1949 some newspapers were calling the exhibition project "Morrison's Folly". It was being called folly to divert scarce resources to build halls and exhibits for pleasure. Building materials were

still in short supply and needed for homes and schools. In the summer of 1950 the Korean War started. Questions were again being raised about whether the proposed "Festival of Britain" should be held. The government persisted. After years of hardship, 1951 was to be a year of "fun, fantasy and colour".

Exhibitions and pageants

A Festival on London's South Bank bomb site was not the only celebration planned. There was to be a travelling exhibition in the provinces as well as pageants of local history in many places. Michael Storm (b.1935) remembers his Yorkshire village pageant, written by the vicar.

On 3 May 1951 the King and Queen went to St Paul's cathedral and declared London's festival open. *The Times* reported the public was in a "joyous mood". Over 8 million people visited the Battersea Pleasure Gardens and nearly 8.5 million went to the South Bank exhibitions. Displays showed crafts such as thatching, as well as how the British Isles were formed. There was a "Gremlin Grange" demonstrating how *not* to build a home (complete with rising damp and burst pipes).

There was even an "Eccentrics Corner" showing visitors just how "mad" the British could be.

Hilary Strudwick (b.1939): "My 14-year-old sister came down from Manchester with a school party and stayed in London a few days. She was amazed by it all." Michael Taylor (b.1936) was fascinated by a metal tower (the "Skylon") that reached high into the sky.

The South Bank Festival was seen by a smaller part of the population than the Great Exhibition of 1851, but the 1951 Festival *was* a welcome distraction. Throughout Britain there were concerts, fireworks, displays, children's sport and other events. The BBC put on nearly 3000 related programmes.

In September 1951 the Festival closed and Britain moved well and truly into a new decade. Labour had won the General Election in February 1950, but with an overall majority of only six. The General Election of October 1951 put the Conservatives into office for the next 13 years.

By 1951, most wartime controls had been lifted. The country was looking forward to brighter times. Michael Taylor (b.1936) remembers the mood of excitement: "Now things were going to be better."

Date List

1944	Education Act.
1945	Second World War ends.
	General Election; Labour landslide.
	Clement Atlee becomes Prime Minister.
1946	Squatters take over former military camps and empty homes.
	New Towns Act.
	National Insurance Act (start of Maternity Grants, Death Grants, Family Allowances...).
	Restrictions on shoe-making removed.
	First post-war "Schoolboys' Exhibition" held.
	Nationalization of Bank of England, coal industry, civil aviation.
	Wartime Council for the Encouragement of Music and the Arts changed into Arts Council.
1947	Royal Wedding of Princess Elizabeth and Lieutenant Philip Mountbatten R.N.A.
	Coldest winter since 1881.
	Potato rationing starts.
	Unusual food "snoek" introduced.
	Start of "New Look" fashion.
	School-leaving age raised to 15.
	Secondary Schools Examinations Council (SSEC) recommends exam system should change.
	Nationalization of electricity industry.
	Sixth World Jamboree of Boy Scouts, in France: "Jamboree of Peace".
1947/8	New teaching aid "filmstrips" introduced.
	Independence of India, Pakistan, Ceylon, Burma.

1948	Marshall Plan aid to Britain and Europe starts.
	Organization for European Economic Co-operation (OEEC) formed.
	British Nationality Act affecting immigration.
	Bread rationing starts.
	First self-service store in UK opens for *food*.
	National Health Service begins.
	Children's Act.
	National Service Act, making National Service compulsory.
	Nationalization of railways, gas, iron and steel industries.
	Criminal Justice Act.
1949	North Atlantic Treaty Organization (NATO) formed.
	Housing Act introduces improvement grants.
	Legal Aid Act.
	End of clothing coupons.
1950	New children's comic, *Eagle,* launched.
	General Election: Labour with overall majority of only six.
1951	First self service store in UK for clothes.
	New GCE exams first held.
	Introduction of "X" certificate, banning children from some films.
	Festival of Britain.
	General Election: Conservatives win, Winston Churchill becomes Prime Minister.
1952	End of price controls on children's wear.

Glossary

bob	slang term for old shilling coin (see shilling below).
coalition	union; coalition government is several distinct parties temporarily joined in governing.
demob	de-mobilize – let out of military service.
evacuation	sending people out of areas likely to be bombed to areas considered safe.
nationalization	government taking over ownership of an industry or service.
pill-box defences	miniature forts put up beside highways and on street corners from which shots could be fired at enemy in case of invasion.
ration	fixed share or allowance of what is available.
shilling	British coin used until early 1970s when decimal coinage started; worth about 5 new pence; 20 shillings equalled one pound.
squatters	homeless people moving into empty property illegally.
tick	slang term for "credit"; "on tick" – getting goods now and paying later.
utility	(clothes or furniture) very basic styles using as little material as possible.
V-E Day	"Victory in Europe Day" war in Europe was formally over on 8 May, 1945.
V-J Day	"Victory over Japan Day" – war with Japan was formally over on 14 August, 1945.

Books for Further Reading

Bartlett, C. J., *A History of Post-war Britain 1945-1974,* Longman, 1977

Longmate, Norman, *How We Lived Then,* Hutchinson, 1971

Madjwick, P. J. and others, *Britain Since 1945,* Hutchinson, 1982

Marwick, Arthur, *British Society Since 1945,* Penguin, 1982

Ryder, J. & Silver H., *Modern English Society,* Methuen and Co., 1977

Seaman, L. C. B., *Post-Victorian Britain 1902-1951,* Methuen and Co., 1966

Sissons, M. and French, P. (eds), *The Age of Austerity 1945-1951,* Penguin, 1963

The author warmly thanks the following for contributing memories to this book:

Bridget Hastie- Smith
(b. 1932)

Roger Iddles
(b. 1942)

Valerie Knight
(b. 1931)

John Owen
(b. 1940)

Gerald Pudney
(b. 1944)

Michael Storm
(b. 1935)

Hilary Strudwick
(b. 1939)

Michael Taylor
(b. 1936)

Derek Walker
(b. 1934)

Index

The numbers in **bold type** refer to figure numbers of the illustrations